GLIMPSES
of the DIVINE

GLIMPSES
of the DIVINE

WORKING WITH THE
TEACHINGS OF SAI BABA

BY
BIRGITTE
RODRIGUEZ

SAMUEL WEISER, INC.

York Beach, Maine

My profound appreciation to Ian Wood who helped me with this
project; and to my son, Niels Kampmann, who guided this book
through to completion.

First published in 1993 by
Samuel Weiser, Inc.
Box 612
York Beach, ME 03910

Library of Congress Cataloging-in-Publication Data

Rodriguez, Birgitte.
    Glimpses of the divine / by Birgitte Rodriguez.
        p.   cm.
    1. Spiritual life. 2. Rodriguez, Birgitte. 3. Sathya Sai Baba,
    1926–   . I. Title.
    BL624.R6275 1992
    294.5'4--dc20   92–23074
                                                        CIP
ISBN 0–87728–766–X
BJ

Cover photograph copyright © 1993 Zenka. Used by kind permission.

Typeset in 11 point Sabon

Printed in the United States of America

The paper used in this publication meets the minimum requirements of the
American National Standard for Permanence of Paper for Printed Library
materials Z39.48–1984.

Contents

Acknowledgments ix
Introduction xi
Steps on the Spiritual Path xiii

Part One : Baba's Teachings

The French Maid 3
A Cultural Shock the Other Way Round 7
The Mother-in-Law 10
Is Sri Sathya Sai Baba God? 13
The Height of Foolishness 16
On Holiday with the Divine in the Mountains of India . 18
The Call 23
A Unique Feature 25
Is Sri Sathya Sai Baba Teaching Religion? 28
The High Commissioner 30
See Divinity in Everything and Enjoy It 33
The Salient Point 37
Surrender 42
Sanathana Dharma 46

Part Two : Baba's Leelas

The Only Criterion 51
Vibhuti 55
Leelas as Lessons 57
Sri Sathya Sai Baba Visits His School in Ooty 61
The Marigold 65
The Art of the Avatar 67
Baba Sends Flowers 69
Another Sign of Grace 71
The Supreme Parent 73
Two Dreams 75

A Drop of Baba's Divinity 78
The White Cobra 79
"Swami, Where Are You?" 81
Political Unrest 83
The Indian Monsoon 86
"See, I Also Have a Kitchen in My Hand" 89
The Last Meal of a Deer 91

Part Three : The Godhead of Parthi

Kodaikanal 95
A Kuja of Water 97
We Could All Pack Up If— 98
The Swiss Clock 100
Baba's Shiva Aspect 103
What is Divine Love? 106
Easwaramma Day 108
A Hindu Wedding 111
The Dance of the Gopis in Modern Times 114
"They Invest in the Soul" 118
Baba's Sankalpa 122
The Doctor of Prasanthi Nilayam 125
A Fifty Rupee Note 126
Evening Talks at Whitefield 128
Puri 135
Life without a Spiritual Ballast Is Not Worth Living 137
A Pilgrimage 140
That Which Holds the Great Subcontinent
    of India Together 147
Taste the Truth 150
A Delightful Morning with Sai at the Hill View Stadium 156
"God is Love, and Love is God" 160
Dasara 162
A Secret Darshan 168
The Divine Visits Bombay 171

The Mother 177
The Divine Flute Player 179

Part Four : A New Way

OM in the Kremlin 185
A New Way 188
The Flowerbeds 194
The Human Mind is in Great Danger 198
The Himalayan Climb 204
A Reading from the *Book of Bhrigu* 212
Celebration of Joy 216
Valedictory Address 219
The New Year 221

Epilogue 228
Glossary 229
Bibliography 233

To Thee, who guides me safely along the mountain path of spiritual life,

To Thee, who gives me such unforgettable moments of joy and inner peace and a sense of absolute security,

To Thee, to whom I owe all,

To Thee, I bow down in deepest gratitude placing at Thy Feet these humble glimpses of life in the sanctuary of Thy love.

Om Sai Ram
Gita

Acknowledgments

In the process of writing this book, I found that I was quoting words from many talks that I have heard Sathya Sai Baba give to students over the years. My quotes are as accurate as possible, considering that I was writing as quickly as I could in a notebook that was ever-present. In my early search in India, I was very much influenced by Sri Aurobindo and The Mother, and have quoted from their publications as well. It is with profound gratitude and appreciation that I have presented material from these great teachers in this book.

Seekers who are on the path may want to explore other material about Sai Baba by visiting his ashram, which is called Prasanthi Nilayam, in Puttaparthi in south India. People wishing to write the ashram should address correspondence to P.O. Anantapur District, A. P. 515134, India. People interested in more literature concerning Sai Baba can write to the Sathya Sai Baba Book Center, 305 West 1st Street, Tustin, CA 92680.

The Sri Aurobindo Ashram is also located in India, and people wishing to go there can write to the Sri Aurobindo Ashram in Pondicherry, India 605002. If readers are interested in locating books by Sri Aurobindo, they can write to Lotus Light Publications, P.O. Box 325, Twin Lakes, WI 53181 for the most up-to-date list of publications available in the USA.

Introduction

Glimpses of the Divine is primarily an account of my experiences in the presence of Sri Sathya Sai Baba, who is guiding the often faltering footsteps of this fragile devotee—sometimes with unflinching sternness, sometimes with infinite sweetness—on the path to self-awareness. I am aware that what Baba has done out of sheer compassion in an attempt to draw this soul closer and perhaps, eventually, is to give it the light and freedom it has always been struggling to achieve. This book is, I hope, the beginning of the end of a spiritual journey that has taken me to many countries and through a variety of religious disciplines and practices, in search of truth and reality.

Sathya Sai Baba is regarded by his 50–60 million devotees around the world as a Poorna Avatar—a manifestation of God in human form with full divine powers—who has command over time, space, and creation itself, and who is, therefore, omnipotent, omnipresent, and omniscient. He was born in the remote southern Indian village of Puttaparthi on November 23, 1926. His principal ashram, Prasanthi Nilayam, is adjacent to the village and has become the center of a vast spiritual, educational and service network that has spread throughout India and to most countries of the world.

One of the difficulties associated with writing a personal account of a spiritual journey is trying to maintain a sense of proportion in the face of persistent, intrusive attempts by the ego to commandeer the project. The ego has very little place in spiritual life. The aim is perhaps not so much its annihilation but its sublimation and eventual transformation. This can take place in various ways: by giving up all desire, for example, for desire is ego; or quite simply by jumping right into the problem and giving oneself unconditionally to the highest Truth, the Divine.

It has been my experience that this latter approach is a more radical way to attempt to annul the superficial ego. Then all desires automatically fall away and there is an inner warmth, a beauty, and a creative life as all work is done for the Divine. There arise brief, rare moments when the self is forgotten—and that in itself is a great relief.

 # Steps on
the Spiritual Path

I was born in Denmark and spent most of my childhood on the family's large country estate. My earliest memories are of the sheer beauty of the countryside, of vast stretches of meadow where hundreds of cows grazed peacefully, of the woods teaming with game, and a lovely stream that formed a natural boundary to the estate.

Evenings were often spent listening to farm workers playing their harmonicas in the last rays of the setting sun while horses, freed of their heavy harness, galloped to the lake to swim in the cool water after a long day in the fields. But despite this idyllic setting, relationships within the privacy of the family were anything but happy. My parents were unable to tolerate each other and rarely spoke, and although my father and mother loved me in their own way, the atmosphere in the home was joyless.

I realized very early in life that something was missing from what was a protected and privileged lifestyle. There was a longing in my heart for something more that I could not fully understand or discuss with others and which grew stronger with the years. The name of God was never mentioned in our family—it was considered poor form to do so—and I found the religion taught at school, with a God sitting high and unapproachable in Heaven meting out reward to the faithful and punishment to the unfaithful, quite meaningless.

My parents, sensing my loneliness and wanting to give me the best education possible, sent me to upper secondary boarding school. I graduated three years later and completed my schooling in Copenhagen, studying German and English. In Copenhagen I met a young man and fell in love. The relationship was to last almost seven years and give me my only child, a son.

During this period, my life seemed flooded with a nameless sorrow and I was on the verge of a nervous breakdown. At this point my parents called me home, and feeling broken in body and soul, I remember receiving a kiss from my father for the first time. Their sympathy and affection helped effect a complete recovery, and I returned to Copenhagen determined to end the relationship. But that proved impossible and ended only when my friend eventually married another woman.

There followed a period when I turned my back on a Scandinavian welfare society and lived alone with my small son, Niels, on a remote country farm, visited occasionally by friends and relatives. It was a time of peace and great simplicity and provided the time to begin corresponding with a guru in the Himalayas who had written a number of books on the Kundalini Shakti. We were eventually to meet.

It was a healthy period for mother and child that was to serve as ballast for the nomadic years of travel that were to follow, for when Niels was 6 years old his father died, and once affairs relating to his estate had been finalized, we left Denmark to begin the search for Truth.

My first stop was Rome. A stay of several months brought the realization that the country's cultural eminence from an earlier epoch was not matched by present day religious observance. Catholicism as practiced in Italy, with a priest from a pulpit high above preaching about sin and hell to a fallen congregation below, did not seem to me to have much to do with spiritual life, or have anything to do with the teachings of Jesus Christ, whom I loved. Finding the same naive reflections in catholicism as in protestantism, I turned to Zen.

The path led to a Buddhist center on the outskirts of Rochester, New York, run by the author of the famous book, *The Three Pillars of Zen*.[1] Although my meditative experiences were not too fruitful, I have fond memories of the beauty of the location and the delight of early morning walks in biting frost, with high snowdrifts piled up along the roads and snowflakes dancing in the light of street lamps. I left Niels in the care of the Rudolf Steiner school in the hills of Vermont and returned to Paris to attend the meditation classes of a Japanese Zen Master. In Zen, a tap on the shoulder with a stick is traditionally used to make the devotee aware that the master finds you dozing—but when, in the absence of the master, a young disciple applied the stick to my back with excessive force, I decided the way of Zen was not for me.

I spent a winter in Zurich, following Selva Raja Yesudian's and Elisabeth Haich's teaching on Yoga, and attending Mrs. Haich's weekly discourses on the ancient wisdom of Egypt at the time of the Pharaohs. Raja Yesudian had, through the Yoga he was teaching, developed his body to a remarkable level of perfection and beauty, and Mrs. Haich's book, *Initiation*, with its central theme of "know thyself," had created quite a stir at the time of its publication in bourgeois Zurich.

The dictates of my inner voice now told me to turn to the East, and I decided to follow. Accompanied only by a suitcase packed with light summer clothes, I boarded a flight for Bombay. My first encounter with India came that evening as I sat down to a sumptuous meal in an expensive hotel. So shaken was I by the abject poverty in the streets outside that my tears made it impossible to continue eating. On retiring

---

[1]Philip Kapleau, *The Three Pillars of Zen: Teaching, Practice, Enlightenment* (New York: Doubleday, 1980).

for the night, however, I felt a strange sacredness in the atmosphere of the country, an utter contrast to the West, and it felt as if my whole being was enveloped in that sacred atmosphere.

The next morning I left for Rishikesh, reputedly one of the holiest places in India. My destination was the Sivananda Ashram, situated on the Ganges River a few kilometers outside Rishikesh, where I was fortunate to be allocated a room in a new guest house. At one point I took the opportunity to visit the Mahesh Yogi's Ashram, on the opposite bank of the Ganges, and was astonished to find the place surrounded by barbed wire.

A friend and I were ushered into a large hall, but found the presence of the Mahesh, seated on a tiger skin on a raised platform, unattractive. We were told we could be given a mantra—after paying a sum of money. Unimpressed by the experience we returned hurriedly to the Sivananda Ashram. During my stay I took a daily morning bath in the Ganges River, for the waters are regarded as holy. High up the river, just as it came down from the Himalayan foothills, a curve in the embankment formed a pool of crystal clear, cool water. A swim in its waters always proved immensely refreshing and recuperative. It was at this ashram that I first heard about Sri Aurobindo and the Mother. Back in Delhi, and intending to return to London, I bought a book by Sri Aurobindo that created such an impression I altered my travel plans and went to Pondicherry in South India, where the Sri Aurobindo Ashram was situated.

I arrived on August 15th—Sri Aurobindo's birthday—for a three-day stay. The ashram looked like an exotic garden, with beautiful flower arrangements everywhere, and the entire setting seemed permeated by light and charged with the highest vibration.

Sri Aurobindo had died in 1950, and his marble tomb was covered with a thick carpet of fresh flowers in two shades of purple, by coincidence the same two shades that were featured in a sari I had just purchased. But five years were to elapse before I was to return to the Ashram, meet the Mother, and stay for many years.

My next spiritual inquiry led me to J. Krishnamurti, whom I followed for four years. On returning to Madras from Pondicherry, I discovered that Krishnamurti was to give some lectures and checked into the Adyar, The Theosophical Society, where a number of his devotees were staying. That evening the venue for the talk was a big private garden, bathed in crimson light from the sun slowly setting on the horizon. There was a condensed atmosphere of something very oriental that warm evening under the stars. Suddenly Krishnamurti came out of the house, a man in his 60s with snow-white hair and a distinguished, elegant appearance. He sat down on a platform, with microphones in front of him, and focused his attention on the audience. Then he began to speak:

". . . There is only one factor, and that is this sense of great compassion. And that compassion IS when we understand the full width and depth of suffering, the suffering not only of a human being, but the collective suffering of mankind.

"Don't understand it verbally or intellectually but somewhere else, in your heart, feel the thing. And as you are the world the world is you, if there is this birth of compassion you will inevitably bring about unity, you can't help it."

Krishnamurti was a great saint who lived what he preached, and at that time, I was fascinated by his personality and teachings. I arranged for my son to continue his schooling at Krishnamurti's Rishi Valley School in India, which Niels said was the best he had ever attended. At the time he did not understand much of Krishnamurti's teachings, but when he left the school he seemed to be able to appreciate the teachings more than I. After India, Niels' education continued in England, where a devotee had bought a large estate south of London that was converted into a school and center for Krishnamurti's teachings. I was not too impressed by the way the school was run. During a visit to England I wrote to Krishnamurti expressing my concerns, and his secretary subsequently rang to arrange a personal meeting with Krishnaji.

My son, Niels, met me at the entrance to Krishnamurti's house and anxiously inquired if I was feeling nervous. I must admit I felt some trepidation at the prospect of meeting this great man, who had followers all over the world. I was shown into a hall as Krishnamurti descended a broad flight of stairs, his slender figure looking picturesque in a pair of blue jeans and a red sweater, and his snow-white hair adding to the impression of someone seeming to step out of a fairy tale. We talked for an hour in the elegantly furnished room, with Krishnamurti seated on a hard wooden chair apparently especially meant for him. He started by saying if anyone else had written him such a letter about the school, it would have gone straight into the wastepaper basket. But he seemed unable to change the present state of affairs, saying, "I have no responsibility for this school." However, my clear impression from his conversation was that he was not too happy about the school either. At the end of the interview he spontaneously took my hand and held it silently in his for quite some time. To me it seemed his way of showing his sympathy with both mother and student, and I left feeling very moved by his nobility.

As the years passed, Krishnamurti began talking over my head, and although his teachings did not really appeal, he will always remain in my memory as a very beautiful saint. "Observe without the observer" seemed to be his teachings in a nutshell. This is, of course, pure *jnana* (the embodiment of universal wisdom) and the "observer" can be taken to mean the ego. At the time I was not aware of this, although I recognized that Krishnamurti was a great *jnani* (sage).

He did, however, sometimes send me into a state of great bliss during which I was completely oblivious of my surroundings. Once in Amsterdam, after he had given a Sunday morning talk to a large and packed auditorium, I sat on a park bench in that beautiful and clean capital of Holland only vaguely aware of people passing by in their Sunday best. Some even attempted conversation, curious to know how I could seem so absorbed.

During the four years I followed Krishnamurti, I met and married an American artist. It was a short, very painful marriage during which I was often reminded of the words of the Mother of Sri Aurobindo's Ashram, "these artists . . . much of it is barren; when one sees the artist at work he lives in an atmosphere of great beauty, but when one sees the same gentleman at home there is only a very minor resemblance . . ." We divorced in a quiet and peaceful way, in circumstances that allowed it to be settled in no time, as if everything had been prearranged. The famous Swiss astrologer, Kundig, once told me during a horoscope reading, "You will always be protected," and I certainly felt that on this occasion.

Now a new chapter in my life was to begin. I felt alien in the West and the longing for something else, something more, was always with me like a cry from an imprisoned heart. But where to turn? To whom should I pray, because I did not believe in God. My innermost soul felt Indian, and the appeal of Sri Aurobindo's teachings was immense — so I returned to his ashram. At the entrance were two jasmine trees and I felt they received me with open arms.

It was 1972, and the ashram, at Pondicherry on the Bay of Bengal, was still being run by the Mother. I knew very little about her, except that she had been born in France, but the day after my arrival I scribbled a rather casual note; "Mother, may I see you?" Although at that time she had withdrawn from the world, I received an immediate reply; "i.i. the next day at 10:30." An inquiry soon revealed that "i.i." meant an individual interview, rather than filing past the Mother in a long line with other devotees. The Mother's apartment was in the main ashram building, which was surrounded by a high, white wall with pearl gray borders. Next day I somewhat nervously walked up a long flight of red carpeted stairs to find many devotees waiting in an anteroom. On entering her apartment I encountered intensely elevating vibrations, and I instinctively knew that here lived a great divinity. The Mother was sitting in a chair on a pedestal looking infinitely superior to all that surrounded her, yet radiating such gentleness. In her hand she held a white rose — a symbol of purity according to her naming of flowers — which she gave to me. I was asked to kneel and place my head on a cushion on the Mother's lap. She began gently stroking my hair. No words were exchanged. According to the Mother, "Words reduce, limit, harden, take away the suppleness and true strength — the life."

For the first time in my life I had met someone whom I intuitively and instantly knew and felt was truly and genuinely Divine. The Mother filled me with her Divine light. I could literally feel it descend into me. But the feeling of light was not all that happened that day. It seemed as though the Mother must surely have performed some kind of "operation" on me. She said, "I go straight in and what has to be done I do. And the moment when I know exactly, you see, I do this (she gestured) quite slowly from above. I see very well, very well, exactly the condition in which each one is." I felt this was exactly what had happened. The Mother had "gone straight in and done what had to be done."

As I left the Mother I was too overcome, for the moment, to go out among the other devotees, although all of them were kind and disciplined and living the Mother's teachings. Instead, I went out onto the Mother's verandah to be alone and sat down in the shade of the huge banyan tree growing at Sri Aurobindo's tomb. Its branches reached up over the Mother's verandah on the second floor. Sitting there I felt completely turned upside down, as if my inner being had done a somersault. It was probably what the Mother called a "psychic opening," when the soul opens to the Mother's touch. Such an avalanche of whatever it was poured down over me — so intensely it translated itself into a sense of unity with everyone and everything, even a blade of grass.

The Mother taught that the individual self and the universal self are one; in every world, in every being, in each thing, in every atom is the Divine Presence, and our mission is to manifest it. Intuitively, without really being aware of it, I *felt* the truth of this statement. As I sat, I leaned my head against one of the branches of the banyan tree and placed my hand on it. To my utter amazement, I felt in the branch small beats, like a human pulse, but infinitely stronger. I took hold of the branch repeatedly, but there was no mistake, each time I felt the steady pulse of the tree. My whole being was filled with a sense of such gratitude that the Divine really existed, that there was something in the universe which was Divine, that tears ran freely down my face. I was simply unable to stop them.

After this first interview, I was granted another three interviews by the Mother during what was to be the last year of her sojourn on Earth. On one occasion I felt the Mother's light, or force, come down into me even more clearly. For some probably subconscious reason, it could only get down to my knees, where it met some resistance. Afterward, as I walked up a flight of stairs, I had to lift each leg, one after the other, using both hands under each knee. I was rather alarmed for a time, but by evening everything had returned to normal.

Sri Aurobindo once wrote about the fact that when we are in the process of spiritualization, we begin to move away from the brilliant poverty of the intellect. Perhaps something like that was happening to me. I found myself more and more in tune with those words, although it was not always easy to follow the teachings, given the intellectual heights in which Sri Aurobindo moved. But for many years, as others read the Bible, I would read Sri Aurobindo, and I made sure that whenever I traveled I always had one of his books with me. His words were immensely inspiring and uplifting. On reading them any gloom I felt immediately changed to high spirits.

On November 24, 1926, Sri Aurobindo withdrew into seclusion to devote his life to his supramental Yoga, and it was in that year that his ashram was founded by the Mother. But November 24, 1926 was also a great day in the life of Sri Aurobindo and regarded by his disciples as equal in importance to his birthday. It was on that day that the descent of the Higher Power, symbolic of the victory of his mission, took place.

As Sri Aurobindo wrote in his book, *Sri Aurobindo on Himself*, "It was the descent of Krishna into the Physical" which rendered possible "the descent of the Supermind" in Matter.[2] It was this, in fact, that was the aim of Sri Aurobindo's Yoga. In a letter to a disciple he said, "The supramental descent is necessary for a dynamic action of the truth in mind, vital and body. This would imply as a final result the disappearance of the unconsciousness of the body, it would no longer be subject to decay and disease."

"It is a higher truth I seek," Sri Aurobindo wrote to another disciple. "Whether it makes men greater or not is not the question, but whether it will give them truth and peace and light to live in and make life something better than a struggle with ignorance and falsehood and pain and strife."[3]

From the beginning of November, 1926, the pressure of the Higher Power began to be unbearable. The great day came on November 24. The Mother knew that a momentous descent had taken place and immediately sent word that all the *sadhakas* (spiritual aspirants) should assemble on Sri Aurobindo's verandah. Mr. A. B. Purani, one of those

---

[2]Sri Aurobindo, *Sri Aurobindo on Himself* (Pondicherry, India: Sri Aurobindo Ashram Trust, 1985), p. 136.
[3]Sri Aurobindo, *Sri Aurobindo on Himself*, p. 143.

present at the time to receive the Master's benedictions, later described the scene: "There was a deep silence. . . . Many saw an oceanic flood of Light rushing down from above. Everyone present felt a kind of pressure above his head. The whole atmosphere was charged with some electrical energy. . . . With a slow dignified step the Mother came out first, followed by Sri Aurobindo with his majestic gait. . . . The Mother sat on a small stool to his right. Silence absolute."[4] The Mother explained afterward that, "Krishna on that day descended into the physical to join and help Sri Aurobindo in this work."

In *Sri Aurobindo on Himself* Sri Aurobindo wrote, "Krishna, . . . the cosmic Deity, Master of the universe, . . . was the guide of my yoga and with whom I realised identity. . . . X thinks I am superior in greatness, you think there can be nothing greater than Krishna: each is entitled to have his own view or feeling, whether it is itself right or not. . . . If you reach Krishna you reach the Divine; if you can give yourself to Him, you give yourself to me."[5] It should be quite clear from this quotation that what happened on November 24, 1926 related to Sri Aurobindo. Quite often Sai devotees take this statement by Sri Aurobindo to be a reference to Sathya Sai Baba who was born on the preceding day, November 23, 1926. It is an incorrect interpretation.

Dr. Gokak, a former vice-chancellor of the Sri Sathya Sai Institute of Higher Learning, once asked Baba, "How come there are two Avatars on Earth at the same time?" Baba promptly replied, "I am LOKANATH and Sri Aurobindo is VYAKTINATH." Thus He indicated that He was Lord of the collectivity, and Sri Aurobindo Lord of the individual. Sri Aurobindo died at the age of 76, when Baba was 24 years old.

---

[4]A. B. Purani, *Evening Talks with Sri Aurobindo* (Pondicherry, India: Sri Aurobindo Ashram Trust, 1982).
[5]Sri Aurobindo, *Sri Aurobindo on Himself*, p. 136, 137.

Sri Sathya Sai Baba has long been acknowledged by his devotees as a manifestation of the many sided Krishna figure, the transcendent Godhead. The Godhead who was incarnate at Brindavan (the forest of Brinda, near Mathurā, where Lord Krishna played in his childhood), and Kurukshetra (the battleground where Arjuna, aided by Krishna, fought the forces of King Dhritarashtra, as told in the Bhagavad Gita), the highest Truth and Consciousness and above all, Immanent in the heart of all creatures. All three — Sri Aurobindo, the Mother, and Baba — represent the same infinitude of the spirit.

By 1926, Sri Aurobindo had already written a vast number of books, including his masterpiece *The Life Divine*.[6] His works, which were described by the Mother as universal and immortal, are wonderfully positive and all based on the same spiritual principle — to aspire to and live the Divine here on earth and not in some high heaven. But Sri Aurobindo's retirement did not mean that he ceased taking an interest in the affairs of the world. An old disciple wrote that Sri Aurobindo kept a close watch on world events and actively intervened whenever necessary, but solely with a spiritual force and a silent spiritual action.[7]

Sri Aurobindo lived in a lovely three-room apartment with a big covered verandah in the main ashram building, and after his death, it was possible to visit the apartment at a certain hour each day. It was so charged with the highest vibrations that devotees involuntarily bowed down to this great Godhead.

In 1938, Sri Aurobindo had an accident. At a moment when, as he said, he was busy protecting the Mother, he fell and sustained a fracture to his hipbone. One outcome of Sri Aurobindo's injury was a change in his retirement that ren-

---

6Sri Aurobindo, *The Life Divine* (Wilmot, WI: Lotus Light Publications, 1990).
7See A. B. Purani, *Evening Talks with Sri Aurobindo* (Pondicherry, India: Sri Aurobindo Ashram Trust, 1982).

dered him available to a small number of close disciples who attended him. For the next twelve years, these disciples had the benefit of informal talks with Sri Aurobindo, and one of them—A. B. Purani—carefully noted and produced these talks as the book called *Evening Talks with Sri Aurobindo*.[8]

Mr. Purani wrote that it was far more important to have the personal contact and the influence of the Master, along with the Divine atmosphere he emanated—for through his outer personality it was the Divine Consciousness that he allowed to act. There was the influence and presence of the Divine.

> The long period of the Second World War with all its vicissitudes passed through these years. At the beginning he did not actively concern himself with it but when it appeared as if Hitler would crush all the forces opposed to him and Nazism would dominate the world, he began to intervene. It was a priceless experience to see how he devoted his energies to the task of saving humanity from the threatened reign of Nazism.
>
> It was a practical lesson of solid work done for humanity without any thought of return or reward, without even letting humanity know what He was doing for it! Thus he lived the Divine and showed us how the Divine cares for the world, how he comes down and works for us.[9]

Sri Aurobindo was also said to be behind British Prime Minister Winston Churchill's forceful speeches to the world as the Germans invaded European countries. At the time, my

[8]A. B. Purani, *Evening Talks with Sri Aurobindo* (Pondicherry, India: Sri Aurobindo Ashram Trust, 1982).

[9]A. B. Purani, *Evening Talks with Sri Aurobindo* (Pondicherry, India: Sri Aurobindo Ashram Trust, 1982), p. 13.

father was living in a country occupied by the Germans, and he saw many of its best men killed. He would sit with his ear glued to the radio whenever Churchill spoke. The rest of the family would also gather in the drawing room to listen with great attention, and a thrill went through everyone when Churchill's voice came across the airwaves. This great statesman helped save the world from the gloomiest disaster—when "the hordes of German Nazis" threatened to invade it.

Mr. Purani wrote in his book, "I shall never forget how Sri Aurobindo who was at one time—in his own words—'not merely a non-cooperator but an enemy of English imperialism' bestowed such anxious care on the health of Churchill . . . it was the work of the Divine, it was the Divine's work for the world.

"It is no exaggeration to say that these Evening Talks were to the small company of disciples what the Aranyakas were to the ancient seekers. Seeking the Light, they came to the dwelling place of their Guru, the greatest seer of the age, and found it their spiritual home—the home of their parents, for, the Mother, his companion in the great mission had come. And these spiritual parents bestowed upon the disciples freely of their Light, their consciousness, their power and their grace."[10]

Here is what Sri Aurobindo himself, the great seer and avatar had to say to humanity, to India, to the individual, and especially the young: "Mother India is not a piece of earth; She is a Power, a Godhead, for all nations have such a Devi supporting their separate existence and keeping it in being.[11]

"It would be a tragic irony of fate if India were to throw away her spiritual heritage at the very moment when in the rest of the world there is more and more turning towards her

[10]A. B. Purani, *Evening Talks*, p. 8.
[11]Sri Aurobindo, *Letters on Yoga*, Vol. 1 (Pondicherry, India: Sri Aurobindo Ashram Trust, 1979), p. 424.

for spiritual help and a saving light. This must and surely will not happen. Indian civilization has been the form and expression of a culture as great as any of the historic civilizations of mankind, great in religion, great in thought of many kinds, great in literature, art and poetry, great in the organisation of society and politics, great in craft, trade and commerce.

"We believe that India is destined to work out her own independent life and civilization, to stand in the forefront of the world and solve the political, social, economic and moral problems which Europe has failed to solve, yet the pursuit of which and the feverish passage in that pursuit from experiment to experiment, from failure to failure she calls her progress. Our means must be as great as our ends and the strength to discover and use the means so as to attain the end can only be found by seeking the eternal source of strength in ourselves.[12]

"We say to humanity, 'The time has come when you must take the great step and rise out of a material existence into the higher, deeper and wider life toward which humanity moves. The problems which have troubled mankind can only be solved by conquering the kingdom within, not by harnessing the forces of Nature to the service of comfort and luxury, but by mastering the forces of the intellect and the spirit, by vindicating the freedom of man within as well as without and by conquering from within external nature.

"We say to the nation, 'It is God's will that we should be ourselves and not Europe. We sought to regain life by following the law of another being than our own. We must return and seek the sources of life and strength within ourselves. We must know our past and recover it for the purposes of our future. Our business is to realize ourselves first and to mold everything to the law of India's eternal life and nature.

---

[12]Sri Aurobindo, *The Karmayogin*, Vol. 2 of *The Birth Centenary Library* (Pondicherry, India: Sri Aurobindo Ashram Trust, 1970, 1972), p. 19.

"We say to the individual and especially to the young who are now arising to do India's work, God's work, 'You cannot cherish these ideals, still less can you fulfill them if you subject your minds to European ideas or look at life from the material standpoint. Materially you are nothing, spiritually you are everything. It is only the Indian who can believe everything, dare everything, sacrifice everything. First therefore become Indians. Recover the Aryan thought, the Aryan discipline, the Aryan character, the Aryan life. Recover the Vedanta, the Gita, the Yoga. Recover them not only in intellect or sentiments but in your lives. Love them and you will be great and strong, mighty, invincible and fearless. Neither life nor death will have any terrors for you. Difficulty and impossibility will vanish from your vocabularies. For it is in the spirit that strength is eternal and you must win back the kingdom of yourselves, the inner Swaraj, before you can win back your outer empire.

"There the Mother dwells and She waits for worship that She may give strength. Believe in Her, serve Her, lose your wills in Hers, your egoism in the greater ego of the country, your separate selfishness in the service of humanity. Recover the source of all strength in yourselves and all else will be added to you, social soundness, intellectual preeminence, political freedom, the mastery of human thought, the hegemony of the world."[13]

After Sri Aurobindo's death in 1950, the Mother also founded the Sri Aurobindo International Center of Education. Though devotees in the ashram had little contact with its approximately five hundred students, nonetheless there was the impression of a harmonious young generation growing up in the Center. By 1989 there was a five year waiting time for students to get into the Sri Aurobindo International Center of Education in Pondicherry.

---

[13]Sri Aurobindo, *The Karmayogin*, pp. 20, 21.

The students had a special place in the Mother's consciousness, but they had to work hard. The Mother was stern with them and said that this place is not for lazy folk. They were told again and again that order and discipline were of paramount importance. The Mother illustrated this in various ways, and said that people who don't know how to keep their things in order live in cerebral confusion — their ideas are also in disorder in their heads. She would say that you don't need to speak for ten minutes with people if you can manage to enter their rooms and look into their cupboards. You will know immediately in what state they are if you do this!

The students were asked to be silent and just listen to what the Mother said. "Afterward you will come to know what has happened to you. Do not utter useless words. . . . And then there's all the stupidity. . . . You know, some people can begin to think only when they talk. . . . When they do not speak they do not even think! They are not able to think in silence, so they get into the habit of speaking. But the more one is developed, the more intelligent one is, and the less need to express oneself. It is always at a lower level that one needs to talk."[14]

". . . Outside the Divine all is falsehood and illusion, all is mournful obscurity. In the Divine is life, light and joy. In the Divine is the sovereign peace."[15]

These quotations of the Mother's words are just a few samples of her teachings. They are taken from fifteen volumes of books called *The Mother*, which mainly contain her talks to the students, their teachers, and devotees. Her words are as fresh and alive today as when they were spoken. It is interesting to draw a parallel between the words of these two

---

[14]The Mother, *Collected Works of the Mother*, Vol. 6 (Pondicherry, India: Sri Aurobindo Ashram Trust, 1979–1991), p. 22.
[15]The Mother, *Collected Works*, Vol. 14, p. 12.

great Divinities and the Divinity of our time and the profound influence they have on our age.

In the words of Sri Aurobindo, "The work of the Divine always leads to a profound and powerful change, not only in the ethical but in the social and outward life and ideals of the race. His descent becomes, in the soul of the race, a permanent power for the inner living and spiritual rebirth."[16]

In 1968 the Mother founded the international township of Auroville, named after Sri Aurobindo. The opening ceremony was very auspicious with a handful of soil from practically every country in the world, including Russia, being placed in a beautiful, specially designed urn. A number of architecturally outstanding buildings were constructed — including the Sankrit school, the library, which was built as a pyramid, and the central Mandir (The Mother's temple), which was designed like a globe. The Mandir was still under construction during my time at the ashram, and the township itself went through many birth pangs. When the Mother died five years later, it had still not managed to stand on its own feet.

During the last years of her life, the Mother withdrew from the world, but before that she moved freely among the devotees. According to one devotee, "With her life began each second anew." Indeed, a smile from her filled their hearts with an unexpected sweetness. The ashram doctor wrote, "She didn't spare herself for one single second, food and sleep (the Mother never slept, only her body rested) were quite insufficient to come up to her superenergy." After her withdrawal she gave *darshan* (the act of grace that allows devotees to see and be in the presence of a Divine personality) only four time a year from a balcony on the second floor of an ashram building. An immense crowd came for this. During the few minutes she appeared, the highest and most powerful vibrations were surely brought down upon Earth, and

---

[16]Sri Aurobindo, *Sri Aurobindo Birth Centenary Library*, Vol. 13, p. 161.

at that moment there was complete silence. But after the Mother had left the balcony, a veritable whirlwind of talking broke loose.

On one such occasion after darshan the Mother was said to have been crying. Later she said, "Here was this unique possibility and human beings had just such a childish little picture of it. . . . It is rare in the history of Earth that there is a moment like this. . . . There are long intervals between such moments in earthly life, and if the moment is not used . . . ."

Swami has said that when one talks or allows the mind to be distracted after darshan, the energy he has given out returns to him unused, and the person or people have wasted a unique opportunity.

Sri Aurobindo once said that the Divine has no preferences or dislikes and is equal to all, but that does not prevent there being a special relationship with each. The more pure the soul, the easier the access to the Divine; the more developed the nature, the more possibilities. Sri Aurobindo also wrote:

> But when the hour of the Divine draws near,
> The Mighty Mother shall take birth in Time
> And God be born into the human clay
> In forms made ready by your human lives.[17]

Behind her burning heart that longed for progress the Mother was, above all, love. In her *Prayers and Meditations* she wrote, "Let me be a vast mantle of love enveloping all the earth, entering all hearts, murmuring in every ear Thy divine message of hope and peace."[18]

"Thy love is vaster than the universe and more lasting than all the ages; it is infinite, eternal, it is Thyself. And it is

---

[17]Sri Aurobindo, *Savitri: A Legend and a Symbol*, Book II (Pondicherry, India: Sri Aurobindo Ashram Trust, 1987), canto 1, p. 705.

[18]The Mother, *Prayers and Meditations* (Pondicherry, India: Sri Aurobindo Ashram Trust, 1979), p. 136.

Thyself I want to be and that I am, for such is Thy law, such is Thy will."[19]

The Mother's love was so formidably strong that devotees felt obliged to do their best, and if that love reached them during a moment that they were at their worst, there was always this gentle message: "Don't you know that the noblest forces sometimes put on the most impenetrable veil of matter. . . . It is because of the worst, that the best can be founded, and it is because of the best, that the worst can be changed."

The Mother's love for India was strong. She said, "United India has a special mission to fulfill in the world. Sri Aurobindo laid down his life for it and we (the Mother) are prepared to do the same. But, unfortunately, in her blind ambition to imitate the West, India has become materialistic and neglectful of her soul."[20]

"India is the country where the psychic law can and must rule, and the time has come for that here. Besides, it is the only possible salvation for this country whose consciousness has unfortunately been distorted by the influence and domination of a foreign nation but which, in spite of everything, possesses a unique spiritual heritage."[21]

When speaking of a United India, the Mother is referring to India, Pakistan, and Bangladesh. She described the partition of the three countries as England's "farewell gift"(!) when it withdrew from India in 1947. Sri Aurobindo was also against India's partition, seeing the three countries as one body. He often said they must be united again.

During the Mother's last year in the ashram, when she was still presiding over it, the atmosphere was exceedingly beautiful. The dining room, always spotlessly clean, provided excellent, nourishing food for some 2000 devotees and visitors each day. The Mother was loved by all. Her words

---

[19] The Mother, *Prayers and Meditations*, p. 153.
[20] The Mother, *Collected Works*, Vol. 13, pp. 362, 374.
[21] The Mother, *Collected Works*, Vol. 13, p. 378.

were law, and her wish was carried out instantly with implicit obedience to her will and the greatest possible skill. It was as if the whole ashram were bathed in the Mother's light, which according to Sri Aurobindo, was as white as a diamond. It seemed that she watched over every individual *sadhak* (follower) and held each one in her consciousness—a very safe place to be.

The Mother once said, "I am with you because I am you or you are me. I am with you and that signifies a world of things, because I am with you on all levels, on all planes, from the supreme consciousness down to my most physical consciousness. Here in Pondicherry you cannot breathe without breathing my consciousness. It saturates the atmosphere almost materially, in the subtle physical, and extends to the lake, ten kilometers from here. . . . My consciousness can be felt in the material, vital, then on the mental plane and the other higher plane, everywhere."[22]

At the age of 95, still very young in mind, the Mother left her body. It was November 17, 1973. Condolence telegrams streamed in from all over the world, a reflection of the range and diversity of people around the globe who had come to see her. During her long life, the Mother granted interviews to many prominent people. Among them were such celebrities as Pope Paul VI, the Prime Minister of India, Jawaharlal Nehru, and his daughter, Indira Gandhi, who visited several times when she was Prime Minister. The American industrialist Henry Ford also announced his wish to see the Mother. He wanted to know what happened after death, but he died before he could make the trip. The daughter of the American President Woodrow Wilson stayed at the Sri Aurobindo ashram for a considerable period.

In one of her last darshans from the usual balcony, the Mother, holding on to the banisters, leaned forward and looked me straight in the eyes as I stood directly beneath her.

---

[22]The Mother, *Collected Works*, Vol. 13, p. 75.

At that moment everything vanished—my travels, accumulated knowledge, even my thoughts. My mind was completely still. It was a strange, yet lovely feeling. [At the time I was not aware that the activity of the mind has to cease to allow space for higher things to come down into it.] There is a need to go beyond the mind, but how can the mind go beyond itself? Only great teachers, using their Divine powers can help the student achieve this. The Mother had this power, but now she was no longer there.

For several days after the Mother's death, an endless line of people filed past to pay her their last homage. I slipped through the back door before the ashram gates were opened, to stand by her bed. I found her whole body bathed in a golden light. She looked full of eternal peace. I felt very clearly that the Mother had guided me through every step on the inner plane, and that with her ever-watchful eye, she had protected me and even on one occasion, saved my life. As I said a last farewell to the one I regarded as my true Mother— my physical mother had never understood my spiritual longings—tears of grief filled my eyes and rolled uncontrollably down my face. Again and again I wiped them away, but still they came. I had always felt deep down in me was a place where the falsehood of this world could not reach. The Mother had found that place and made it vibrate with life and sweetness. She had pointed out the way, and now it seemed lost. How was I to find it again?

The Mother's departure left a big vacuum at the ashram, but I stayed on for a number of years—taking part in ashram activities and making occasional visits to the West. I also started translating the works of the Mother and Sri Aurobindo. Once confined to a few buildings in one corner of Pondicherry, the Ashram's growth has caused it to expand physically in all directions. Today Ashramites live and work in more than 400 buildings spread throughout the town. The central focus of the community is one group of houses including those in which Sri Aurobindo and the Mother dwelt for most of their lives in Pondicherry. This interconnected block of houses—called "the Ashram main-building," or more usually just "the Ashram"—surrounds a tree-shaded courtyard. At the center of the courtyard lies the flower-covered "Samadhi." This white marble shrine holds, in two separate chambers, the mortal remains of Sri Aurobindo and the Mother.

At the common kitchen, food is prepared three times a day. Rice, vegetables, and fruits are grown on various farms, fields, and gardens belonging to the ashram. A separate kitchen called "Corner House" is run for the students and teachers of the Center of Education. Medical care is available at various clinics staffed by physicians of the allopathic, homoeopathic, ayurvedic and naturopathic systems. There is also a dental and eye clinic, and a department specializing in physiotherapy, massage, and acupuncture. The Reception Service looks after the needs of visitors and arranges accommodations for them in the Ashram's guest houses. The Ashram fosters a variety of artistic and cultural activities. There is a theater for dramatic and other performances and an art room where both Indian and Western music is played. The Ashram's large library is utilized both by students of the Center of Education and by Ashram members, a number of whom are involved in literary activities and research. A separate Archives and Research Library has been established to preserve the manuscripts of Sri Aurobindo and the Mother, and to prepare material for publication.

At present, the Center of Education has about 150 full or part-time teachers and 450 students, ranging from nursery to advanced levels. The curriculum includes the humanities, languages, fine arts, sciences, engineering, technology, and vocational training. Facilities include libraries, laboratories, workshops, a theater, and studios for dance, music, and painting. In 1981, I left the ashram for good. I had been there since 1972. For some reason, I woke one morning and received a clear command to leave—there was not the least doubt in my mind as to what to do. I wondered later whether this could have been the influence of Sri Sathya Sai Baba. Before evening on that day, everything had been donated to friends, and I left early next morning in an Ashram car for Madras airport. From there I flew to Copenhagen with no plans for the future and not knowing what it would bring. I was content to leave everything in the hands of providence. As a parting gift, a spacious apartment designed by my son, who at age 29 worked as a successful architect in New York, was donated to the Ashram.

I had met Baba earlier in 1981 during a brief visit to his ashram, and although I had by no means surrendered to him, I somehow felt a peculiar inner relationship with him. In fact I had not been able to see a picture of Sai Baba in the township of Pondicherry without struggling to hold back tears.

It is to repay, in however small a degree, the debt I owe to Sri Aurobindo and the Mother that material about these two great Divinities has been incorporated in this book. It is also in the hope that others may get a glimpse of the truth of their delightful teachings and share my experience of their blessings.

PART ONE

BABA'S TEACHINGS

The
French Maid

I was still living in Sri Aurobindo's Ashram in Pondicherry when I experienced Baba's first *leela*—the word used to describe the divine play or divine sport of the Lord. The events leading up to the incident gave no clue to the surprise Baba had in store for me.

During a short visit to Copenhagen I heard a program on Danish radio about Sai Baba that sounded interesting. I decided that on the way back to Pondicherry, I would detour via Puttaparthi and find out for myself if he really was the Divinity he was reputed to be. I recalled that once in Gstaad, Switzerland, while attending talks being given by J. Krishnamurti, I had met a lady who had been to see Baba. She described how Baba had placed an apple in her lap, which he appeared to have taken out of thin air. On hearing this, I was skeptical and confused and quite unsure as to whether Baba's teachings were meant for me. So on returning to India, I flew south to Bangalore and undertook a strenuous journey by car over rough country roads to Puttaparthi, a small village in the heart of South India surrounded by a range of hills in a beautiful, serene landscape. This secluded spot is Baba's birthplace and the site for his main ashram.

In spite of fatigue after the long journey from Copenhagen to Puttaparthi, I clearly felt the enormous difference between the outside atmosphere and that of the ashram. It acted like a soothing balm on my tired nerves. Several years

later I heard Baba, during one of his discourses, speak precisely about the atmosphere in the Ashram. He said: "There
is a concentration of Divine consciousness in this ashram."
Obviously this is what I felt without knowing it at the time.
Later, as a resident of the ashram, I heard a constant chanting
of mantras that echoed around the hills, now and again inter-
rupted by a man's clear voice giving instructions. I assumed
they were probably vedic mantras chanted in that way to
purify the atmosphere of the ashram. The chanting took
place each time Baba gave a talk in the vast Poornachandra
hall. The atmosphere was first purified by the recitation of
some powerful vedic mantras sung by students from Baba's
schools and colleges.

My first arrival at the ashram was just at the time when
evening *bhajans* (traditional Indian devotional songs) had
commenced, and it seemed that even the birds in the trees
around the mandir area (main temple) joined in. I didn't see
Baba that first day, but next morning I walked straight into
the compound that surrounded the Mandir to see that Baba
had already come out to give *darshan*. In those early days
there was no need, as there is now because thousands of
devotees constantly arrive to see Baba, to line up outside the
compound in orderly rows and draw lots to see which rows
will take front place.

At first I only saw Baba's back as he talked to a lady on
the opposite side of the compound, but I was immediately
struck by the graciousness of his appearance. Suddenly,
abruptly, he turned around and his glance seemed to come
directly to me right across the compound. I thought it strange
that he should be so aware of a newcomer. Shortly after,
when he reached the place where I, somewhat reservedly, was
sitting, he looked straight into my eyes. Gone, at that
moment, were all doubts and reservations. I knew then,
immediately, that he was the Divine. He sent what seemed
like an electric current right through me. I recall going out
into the village after darshan to buy a few essentials, but

being only able to speak in a whisper. For the rest of the day, I was hardly able to speak a word.

About a week later, Baba left for Whitefield, near Bangalore, which is the location of one of his educational institutions where he also maintains a residence and guest quarters. In those days there was no taxi service at Puttaparthi, but someone managed to hire a ramshackle old car from a local resident that allowed a group of us to follow Baba to Whitefield. As much of our luggage as possible was stacked on the roof, then five of us, together with the remaining baggage, crammed inside the car. The crush was so great the doors couldn't close, so they were tied together with rope. We set out, on bald tires, for the four-hour drive to Whitefield. In my mind I held onto Swami all the way, and thanks to his grace we all arrived safely with no breakdowns en route.

For Baba's first darshan at Whitefield the next day, along with many other devotees, I bought a garland of flowers at the ashram gate to give him. I was able to sit in the front line and as Baba came to the place where I was sitting I handed the garland to him. He did not take it, but instead bent down, and with a force that I felt inwardly, put both his hands on the garland, blessing it and me. Only afterward did I realize that this was not his usual style, which I learned was usually to either lightly touch or not touch at all what was offered to him. A few days later I left for where I felt I belonged, the Sri Aurobindo Ashram. Although I had no intention of returning to Sai Baba, I left with a heavy heart. But then occurred the first leela that I believe I knowingly experienced.

For a number of years I had employed a faithful and honest French servant who, unfortunately, had been an alcoholic for the past thirty years. To put it mildly, it was anything but pleasant when she arrived in the mornings not too sober. But to sack her would have meant that her only means of support was the begging bowl. It was not something I was prepared to consider. She was well-known in our part of town for her habit, and it was all the more pitiful because she was otherwise always tidy and neat and an excellent worker.

On returning from Puttaparthi I was astonished to find that my French maid had given up drinking altogether. The complete change in her was noticed by everyone, and from then on I began to look at Baba's leelas with much more understanding. Later I realized that leelas on the scale being performed by Baba are a natural power for such a Divinity or Godhead. I came to understand that in this Kali Yuga, when it is very difficult for human beings to believe in any Godhead without some tangible proof, Baba must use this power if he wants people to listen to his words, let alone begin to live them. As Sai Baba himself says about his leelas, "They are my visiting cards."

A Cultural Shock the Other Way Round

Westerners visiting India often say they get a "cultural shock" at their first encounter with this country—the enormous over-population in the big cities, people sleeping on pavements, the terrible poverty, dirt and squalor, the huge crowds, the seemingly spontaneous violence, and the entrenched corruption. For me however, having lived so many years in India, it was just the other way around as I struggled to find my feet in the West. For the past fifteen years I had paid only short visits to the culture into which I was born, and my return provided a unique chance to gain a deep insight into the pattern of people's lives in a modern Western society. Indeed, everything had changed so enormously, returning "home" was a "cultural shock."

It depends, of course, on what is considered as culture. In my country—Denmark—there was tremendous efficiency, craftsmanship, and expertise. All aspects of daily life were at a high standard, everything functioned well, cleanliness was the rule, and an outstretched hand begging for money or food was simply unknown. But I found there was a reverse side to this glittering coin—in every walk of life it seemed it was "me first"—always "me first." I came across genuine unselfishness so rarely that when it did appear, it flashed like a ray of sunshine through dark clouds.

To my "eastern" eyes, the warehouses and shops were full; there was a fantastic supply of goods, and despite prices being high, people bought mountains of food. At festival times, such as Christmas, this would take on even more excessive proportions. A sacred feast, during which the highest vibrations of peace descend upon earth, was turned into a charade. The media appealed almost exclusively to people's lowest instincts, and the only guideline for journalism in the midst of such fantastic welfare seemed to be the more banal the better. There is no doubt that we Danes are one of the most spoiled people in the world. But are Danish people — or any one else in the West — happy in general or at least enjoying this great good fortune? My answer is "no." The look on people's faces spoke its own language about a deep boredom. No one seems satisfied. The general attitude is that of constant spoken or unspoken criticism of everybody and everything. This is harmful to those to whom criticism is aimed, as well as those who send such negative thoughts out into the atmosphere.

Many people have reached a point where they can no longer cope — the final irony is to take out a bank loan to pay for the costly process of modern psychoanalysis. The younger generation is unemployed by the thousands, and a walk in one of the city's well kept parks in spring or summer finds young people sitting on benches drinking beer — and their empty cans litter the area. Life seems so petty and shallow, that young people try to get together and live in independent communities, disgusted with the hypocrisy and pretension that surrounds them. They have turned their backs on society, but have formed for themselves another kind of society that is no better. The younger generation feels an aimlessness in life, an inner emptiness. They say, "I want to find something — not God for that is a provincial idea — but something real." If they only knew what India has to offer, I believe they would fall upon it with all the fervor and enthusiasm of youth. In India they could discover peace of mind and that life has purpose.

After about six months in the West, Baba called me back through a strong inner connection. It was a relief to be back in India. As soon as the aircraft landed in Bombay, I again felt that India was a sacred country. India is very beautiful with its endless variety and charm, with its rivers and deserts, the rich red soil, the forests, the palm trees, the parrots and monkeys, the villagers struggling with poverty, the snowclad mountains, and the cool, fresh air in the high country. As I traveled by taxi back to Puttaparthi, it is no exaggeration to say that each tree along the road felt like a blessing.

The Mother-in-Law

At the height of the hot season at Puttaparthi, when the mid-summer sun literally bakes the ashram oven-hot and the heat becomes almost intolerable, particularly for Westerners, many depart for the cooler temperatures found in the mountains. It was during one such summer, when Baba was neither at Puttaparthi or Whitefield and all the school colleges were closed for the summer holidays, that I decided to head for the mountain resort of Ooty. Although it was the high season there, after some difficulty I was able to find a flat to rent for a couple of months.

I had brought a stack of books with me from the ashram bookstore, and I immediately started work on a compilation of Baba's teachings entitled *On the Threshold to a New Era*. I worked night and day for the simple reason that after a few days, a peaceful night's sleep became almost impossible. There were rats in the bathroom, mice in the dressing room, and the living room/bedroom was infested with bugs that appeared to be living in the old wooden floor, the woolen blankets, and anywhere else they could make a home. I was so badly bitten by these small creatures, that I consulted a local skin specialist. He diagnosed an allergy to the particular insect, or "microscopic fly," as he called it. Unfortunately, the medicine he prescribed to ease the terrible itching only made it worse! The hosts of the place did their best to ease the intolerable situation. They frequently invited me to dinner and even gave their dog a bath (probably for the first time in its life) in case it was carrying bugs.

I was unable to move because no other accommodation was available at that time of year, and the prospect of returning to the 104 degree temperatures at the ashram held no appeal. I was stuck with my situation, and before long my nerves were well and truly frayed!

I ventured out to the local bazaar several times a week to buy fresh fruit and vegetables, and in my miserable condition, I was ready to assume that shopkeepers doubled and even tripled their prices when they saw me coming. In reality they may or may not have done this—it is not uncommon in India for prices to rise when the customer has a pale skin— but I was, nonetheless, rather severe on these poor people.

After about two months, my work compiling the book was completed, and I returned to Whitefield where Baba was back in residence. One day at darshan, as I sat in the front line, Baba passed by and looked at me with a mischievous smile. He spoke in Telugu, the local language where Baba was born, and said to a young girl sitting next to me, "She is your mother-in-law." I asked the girl if she was certain the remark was about me. She replied that she was "positive" it was intended for me.

At the time I was unable to understand the significance of his remark—only a few months later did it dawn on me what Baba had meant. Mothers-in-law are notoriously difficult to get along with, and a mother-in-law is often regarded as a pretty severe person. That summer I had behaved in a pretty severe way—at least to the shopkeepers in the market at Ooty! I have since taken great care that Baba should have no reason to call me by that name again—nor has he.

To me this little episode showed Baba's omniscience. I was in Ooty, and he was hundreds of miles away, and yet he knew what transpired, and he corrected me in an effective manner, as is his style. He shows people their defects in order to help them improve, and in my experience most of the time the people do improve. Baba often tells his devotees, "Please do not incur the expense of coming to Puttaparthi from wherever you are, whenever you call me, I am ever alert to respond, ever ready to listen and reply." It is a truth I have often experienced.

Is Sri Sathya
Sai Baba God?

It makes sense to attempt to clarify some of Baba's statements and some of the questions that are made about Baba and his nature and identity. Foremost of all these questions must surely be: Is Sri Sathya Sai Baba God?

He himself maintains that he is and many accept this statement without further investigation. There are, however, many others, particularly very religious Italians, who feel confused. They feel the concept "creates a conflict in their minds." Others deny the belief flatly, perhaps because they don't know what is implied in it, or because they grew up in a society that does not prepare them for the meeting of a living Divinity. They prefer to follow their established thought and do not want to be disturbed.

According to most religions, God is a separate being sitting in some high heaven like a dictator. Naturally for all those who believe in this concept of God, Baba's statement that he is God is very confusing! But this model cannot be transferred to Baba. He himself says, "I am in you,"— another statement that many may find difficult to understand.

To my knowledge India is the only country in the world that has a totally different concept of God. Paramahansa Yogananda once said, "We can accurately describe God as Divine Consciousness." And in Baba's own powerful words, "Cosmos has only got one master, God, the all comprehensive highest consciousness." This is the Indian concept of God. From time immemorial India has not only asserted this spiritual truth but also offered various methods to realize it. Nor is this concept a product of speculation, but the result of centuries of investigation by the great Indian rishis and seers.

Whether Baba is God or not depends on which way one looks at the issue. Seen in the light of the Hindu concept of God being the Divine omnipresent and omniscient consciousness, Baba is God manifesting this consciousness in a human form. Then his statement, "I am in you," as all seers and Godmen of India assert, becomes logical for as Baba says "we are all part of this one consciousness." Daily, Baba abundantly proves the truth of this statement in his countless interviews with devotees and nondevotees. He knows each one of us inside and out—our past, our present, and our future. He reads us like an open book. In a recent interview, he said to a married visitor from London, "Where is the other?" causing the man to blush crimson at his pointed question. Baba points out each devotee's *dharma* (right way of living) and he has brought the lives of millions of people back on the right track toward God. It is not likely that there is any other Divine Personality living on Earth today in this dimension of consciousness, as Baba does.

Baba tells us: "Discriminate and decide; dive and declare the depth; eat and judge the taste: that has been the message of the seers of India. Mere axioms without the chance to prove their value to oneself were not thrown at pupils by the ancient preceptors.

"The pupil was told then that Divinity was dancing in every cell of his; that he could therefore be fearless. Meet hatred with your innate prema (love); meet grief with innate joy; meet anger with the shield of santhi (inner peace). You are bound to win.

"Loka is Lokesa (the world is the body of God); the universe is the universal principle manifested in multifarious particulars. Man is Madhava (the divine entity) in miniature.

The human body has been acquired as a gift in return for the meritorious lives spent by you in the past. The nature of man is genuinely divine, in the past, present and future, forever. There was never a time when it was not.

"The Lord is neither in Heaven nor Kailash (the abode of Lord Shiva). . . . To believe that He is manifest only in one place or location and to journey thither is a superstition much to be deplored. He is everywhere, in everyone, at all times. He is the Witness of all, in all. He is the energy that fills space and time and He is the energy that manifests as cause."

The Height
of Foolishness

During a talk given in the mandir (temple) at Prasanthi
Nilayam, Baba explained: "Divine consciousness is God.
This consciousness is permeating everything. It is in an ant as
well as in brahman, only in Brahman it is self-aware forever.
There is nothing in the universe that is not God. How can the
unlimited be limited to a certain form; that is the height of
foolishness. For the sake of human satisfaction you give
name and form to the Lord, but in reality he does not have
any form at all.

"Matter plus energy is God. It is the energy of consciousness that has created the universe. Even in the smallest parti-
cle of matter such as electron, proton, and neutron is this
consciousness. Gold is gold even if it is shaped in all kinds of
ornaments. In the same manner the Divine does not lose its
Divinity because it forms itself in the material universe."

In the Upanishads it is affirmed that: "Brahman is the
One besides whom there is nothing else existent. . . . Brahman is the consciousness that knows itself in all that exists."
That is what Sri Sathya Sai Baba does. He knows himself in
everything and in each and every one of us, as he has assured
us, and proved any number of times — because he is that highest omnipresent Brahman consciousness.

It is further stated in the Upanishads that, "Brahman is
one with our soul and our true soul is our self or atma without which we could not breathe or live." Baba's manifestation

among us thus has profound meaning. He helps us find our own true soul or self, to become self-aware, because he is one with our soul. This self-awareness is a mighty difficult job, but it is all that our sojourn here on Earth is about. All the rest is of secondary importance, a means to help us to this awareness. One cannot, however, attain this awareness without the Divine's guidance, and it is supremely worthwhile to seek. When the Avatar is the teacher the truth is pure and unalloyed.

Baba closed his talk by saying: "Who but a pathfinder, Divine Teacher and savior can save man by leading him to the path of real peace? Who but Him can help to find Madhava in manava (God in man)? Is it possible for an ordinary guru with human failings? Who but an electrical engineer can repair the defects in the mechanism and dispel the darkness with the illumination of electric lights? The Advent of this Avatar is for you. He is sure to guide you along the path to ultimate realization. He will show you the sure knowledge of the self by dispelling all doubts, fears, and sufferings. Once genuine peace reigns in the human heart, once purity of human mind is ensured, peace will prevail on Earth. Remember the Divine call—Through men with pure heart and without animosity, sensual desire, greed and violence, prosperity and peace can come to the world."

On Holiday with the Divine in the Mountains of India

A favorite place to escape the suffocating summer heat of the plains is the beauty of the Indian mountains at Kodaikanal. There the air is pure, cool, and refreshing and it is possible to breathe freely again. The journey is a strenuous one, about ten hours by car from Bangalore. But one of the rewards along the ever-winding road of hairpin curves is the "silver cascade,"—a dazzling waterfall about seven kilometers before Kodaikanal that drops about a thousands meters straight down the sheer mountainside. The last part of its massive fall is softened by protruding rocks. Weary travelers often stop and go fully dressed under the water to take a "shower," thus cleansing themselves of both dust and stress after the long drive. In the peak season at Kodai prices for accommodations are expensive, places to stay difficult to find, and it is often necessary to put up with a number of hardships. But to compensate, there is always the alpine sun and the pure air that have a marvelous, curative effect.

On this particular trip, the rumor that Sri Sathya Sai Baba is coming had spread long before he arrived. A few devotees had already been waiting for some days at the lake-side house he would use during his stay. At last, in the late afternoon I saw a car carrying a number of Baba's guests, among whom were a few Westerners, drive up to the front of the house. After being driven slowly in a red Mercedes Benz, Baba soon arrived.

As the gates of the compound opened, I was only able to catch a glimpse of that wonderful head. He looked tired, having just made a seven-to-eight-hour drive from Ooty, another hill station. About half-an-hour later, a cavalcade of buses, vans, taxis, and private cars began to arrive and pour out their load of dishevelled devotees, all of whom had made a similar journey from Ooty. There was much talking and little doing as everyone waited for an hour, then two hours in the hope that there might be a darshan on that first day. It was not to be. When a small brown hand drew a curtain in one of the windows and Baba appeared in all his simplicity, he went unnoticed by most — unfortunately a hedge obscured a view of him.

After lodgings have been found in Kodaikanal, the next problem for the devotees is transportation, as Swami's house is quite a distance from most lodgings. People solve this in various ways, either sharing a taxi, walking, rowing across the lake, or even renting a bicycle. Leaving a bicycle unlocked in India can be a risky business, and when local people told me that "Kodais do not steal" I accepted the statement skeptically. But it turned out to be true! A good bicycle can be left unlocked anywhere for hours, and it is still there when you return to pick it up. For good measure, I should add, Kodais also don't beg.

During Baba's entire stay, from the first day to the last, from morning darshan to evening darshan and often overnight, a long row of cushions, shawls, and mats are parked along the public road on both sides of the entrance gate to his house. Stones are placed on top to keep these "reserved" seats in place. Young people dressed in rags pass by, but even with no cushion to rest their heads on at night, they never succumb to the temptation to take the seats — despite the great poverty in Kodai. Their hearts, it seems, are more noble than those who "reserve" their seats in this strange manner!

In preparation for the first morning darshan, groups of devotees waited in the delightful gardens in front of Baba's attractively designed house. All eyes were turned toward the entrance door on the terrace. After a while it opened, and like a flame of love, Baba appeared in his red robe. Instantly there was absolute silence. Slowly this *Prema Swarupa* (embodiment of love) began moving among the devotees. A man, sitting to the left, was weeping. In his arms he held his son whose head hung down on his chest. His legs dangled. The boy couldn't talk and looked more dead than alive. Baba poured out all his love and compassion to the poor father, who was granted three consecutive interviews and the promise that his little son would heal and be able to walk and talk. But, Baba added, "His brain is weak."

Baba is known to have cured practically every disease under the sun and has also greatly sharpened the intellectual capacities of some of his students. At least now the father was happy, his face relaxed as he rested within himself. His soul had felt the Divine touch. The atmosphere of the place was charged with the highest vibrations.

A look from Swami penetrated into the innermost recesses of my being and filled my heart with an unspeakable peace and calmness. I left that first darshan to sit in the cool shade of a tall pine tree and enjoy the feeling of serene peace.

Students from the Sathya Sai colleges, lucky enough to have been invited to spend some of their holidays with the Master in the mountains, could be seen leaving the house in the mornings. Equipped with woolen sweaters and cameras, they boarded the college bus for an excursion to one of the many famous viewing places, such as Coaker's Walk. It is an extraordinary lookout that commands a marvelous and breathtaking view of the entire valley, framed by a range of grandiose mountains. Or they took a stroll around the big and beautiful Kodaikanal Lake, which until they disappeared a few years ago, was a happy resort for swans.

This reminds me that humankind is small and frail and allows impurities to contaminate the "lake" of the heart. We must ensure that the "lake" of the mind becomes, and remains, a happy resort for the swans of Soham Thatwa (I am That; the reality). As Baba once said during a discourse at Brindavan, "Man becomes a victim of ignorance, darkness and lust if we give unrestricted freedom to the senses." These students did not behave like that. Their conduct and manner was quite different from that of other young people. They walked briskly along in small groups quietly talking among themselves, looking happy and self-composed. Their great Master had put his seal on them.

At evening darshan, like a blessing, Swami walked among the devotees. There were few, if any, who did not feel that these mountain darshans were something very special as he poured his Divinity over everyone. The contact with Swami on a physical level was much closer than usual because there were no large crowds. At the end of darshan, college students came out onto the terrace with their tutors to sing *bhajans* (chants), which to a remarkable extent purifies the atmosphere. Devotees usually lingered on long after bhajans were over, finding it difficult to leave the holy place charged with shanti (peace).

During this visit to the mountains Swami granted few interviews, but made an exception for a lady from Copenhagen who was suffering from terminal cancer. Although she did not know how much longer she had to live, she was very brave. At the end of the interview, her face was flushed, and she was a little bewildered by Swami's teachings. I recall her saying, "If I let go of my ego and have none, how can I take an interest in life? Would I not become totally indifferent to everything? I would like to take part in life." At that point she had little peace of mind, but knowing she had received help from the Divine, she was soon able to move forward with increasing confidence.

In a discourse at Brindavan, relating in part to the problem of the ego, Baba said: "Indeed selfishness (ego) is essential in the beginning. But you cannot grow spiritually if you are limited to yourself. N. had to face a number of difficulties. He had no peace of mind. The path of self-realization was prescribed for him. In the Bhagavad Gita, Krishna reveals to Arjuna the esoteric but simple path to self-realization for attainment of abiding peace. The immediate, intimate, and intuitive apprehension of the immanent effulgence of divinity pervading the microcosm and the macrocosm is the highest liberating experience. Shut the doors of outward perception and look inward. Transcend the barriers of thought. Travel along the mountain path of life and reach the peak. Come out of the dark night of the soul and divine grace will descend upon you."

Swami stayed ten days in Kodaikanal, and each day of this holiday with the Divine seemed special in its own way. When he departed, those remaining behind were undoubtedly saddened by the loss of his lovely mountain darshans, but they hoped and expected that he would visit again.

The Call

For many years I had heard the call to set out on a spiritual journey—a call once heard that you cannot but follow. But I never dreamed that I would write a book about my experiences. Certainly not a book in English. It would not have been possible if Baba had not followed my work all the way and constantly helped with the endeavor.

Only once has he let me understand that he wanted to see one particular chapter called "The Divine Visits the City of Bombay." It was written, quite literally, at his feet. During a visit to Bombay, someone was giving a talk in Baba's presence that was of no great interest to me—so I decided to get on with my writing. As I sat right in front of him, concentrating on my work and completely unaware of everything else, Baba did not take his eyes off me. Each time I glanced up, I looked into two eyes of unfathomable depth. The chapter was handed to him the next day during darshan, and he acknowledged receipt of it with a smile. Apart from that Baba has not read a single line of the manuscript.

I am aware, however, that he knew each word that was written and gave his encouragement to go on if I felt stranded—as well as showing his disapproval if something was not in tune with the overall content of the book. Those latter pages went straight into the wastepaper basket. The languages the book is written in, whether it is Danish or

English, seems absolutely secondary—he knows the content and shows clearly if it is suitable or not.

For example, I had written a number of unflattering pages about the attitude and behavior of Danish young people and their studies. Without reading a word, Baba indicated very strongly that he disapproved by simply turning his back to me and otherwise ignoring me! After coming to terms with this somewhat severe correction, I took the offending pages out of the manuscript and thanked Baba for his guidance.

On the other hand, if there was something he approved of, I would sometimes find a small, irregular-sized photo of him on the floor in the space that I normally occupied during evening meditation in the temple. My exact sitting position could not have been seen by him physically, because he never came into the temple at that time of day. However the photo arrived, whether Baba simply caused it to materialize or used some other method. To me it was a charming little token of his awareness and appreciation.

In writing *Glimpses of the Divine*, I have tried to be as objective as possible and keep my ego in check—on the grounds that, like everyone else, I am merely an observer of the drama of my own life. Nonetheless, at times the book is inevitably a subjective account of my own personal experiences, and I hope that thereby it is enlivened by an individual color and life that it might not otherwise have had.

It is impossible in mere words to describe a multifaceted Divine Personality, who guides his devotees with such infinite care and protection, as Sathya Sai Baba. It has been my experience and observation that the closer you come to him, the more he showers his grace upon you. It has been my aim to try and convey in these pages a living impression of this great Godhead whose unfailing Masterhand guides those who follow him on the great journey.

A Unique Feature

Puttaparthi is the center for the Sri Sathya Sai Institute of Higher Learning. From this Center inspiration emanates to the rest of the world to incorporate Baba's unique program called Education in Human Values (EHV) into today's educational systems. The aim is to integrate the five universal values—truth, right conduct, love, peace and non-violence—into the teaching of all subjects. Baba has stressed repeatedly that: "Education without character, science without humanity, commerce without morality, and politics without principles are not only useless, but positively dangerous."

Baba is the supreme organizer of this great program and the central personality in the lives of the thousands of students who love and adore him. The change that he brings about in youth—the conduct of their lives—is a unique feature. Discipline is the key word in their education, but it is a discipline brought about by love. The students thrive in the orderly, clean, quiet atmosphere that is a stabilizing influence on young, restless minds in all Sathya Sai Educational institutions.

The students show respect for their teachers and each other, and the tone of voice they use among themselves is friendly and considerate. One of the aims of the student's education is to bring the true person to the forefront, and that true person is the inner self.

Academic standards at the Sathya Sai Institute of Higher Learning, deemed a university by educational authorities in India, are high. All lessons are taught in English. Education at Baba's various schools, colleges, and institutes of higher learning is free and open to all who pass the entrance examination. What seems to differentiate these students from other students around the world is that they are not only academically advanced, but spiritually enlightened. They have consideration for themselves and others, they are disciplined, but above all their actions are based on an awareness of human values. That makes all the difference. It gives the students a feeling of purposeful living that no ordinary school can give. I have talked with many students, male and female, and am always struck by their remarkable self-composure and kind, thoughtful attitudes. It is a conduct that is characteristic of all the students. These young people are privileged to grow up in such a unique and spiritually charged atmosphere. Once they graduate from the Sri Sathya Sai colleges and institutions and go out into the world, all doors seem to open for them. Their efficiency and integrity is well-known throughout India.

Perhaps it is not fair to compare students in the West with Baba's students, yet it is impossible not to notice the enormous difference. While the Sri Sathya Sai institutions base their education on human values, in the West these values are almost completely missing, and the results suffer accordingly.

Much of today's student world is in utter confusion. I am sure, however, that something is stirring beneath the surface that is beginning to affect many of the young people who pass through Western-style systems. The inner emptiness they feel will perhaps one day lead them to an awareness that life is sacred and has a sacred purpose. This awareness will change everything, making life meaningful and allowing all their fine qualities to emerge. The soul behind the outer chaos is beautiful, but it simply can't shine through!

Baba, in his clear and luminous words, has had this to say to today's students and their teachers: "Any system of education that does not help to discriminate between right and wrong, that does not instill the fear of sin and the love of God, train you in the codes of humility and reverence, widen the horizon of your wonder, encourage you to worshipfully serve your parents, and inspire you to dedicate your skills and attainments to the progress of your family, village community, and country stands condemned.

"The corruption and cruelty that are rampant in the world can be traced to such grave defects. Selfishness, greed, pomp and injustice are prevalent in every field. The nations have no peace and the sense of security is feeble. As science develops and technology advances, humility and mutual love should also develop to the same extent, otherwise man becomes a menace to man. Human sensitivity must be so high that no one can tolerate the misery of others."

Is Sri
Sathya Sai Baba
Teaching Religion?

Religion conveys the idea of faith, and faith may change—a Hindu may change his faith to become a Muslim, a Christian may become a Buddhist. But Baba's teachings rest on the eternal Truth. His mission, in his own words, is to revive dharma (right conduct; the way to higher life) for all humanity. And Baba has indicated that dharma is beyond religion or creed, "Dharma is to follow the path of Truth."

Swami has also stated, "I have come to carry out the supreme mission of spiritually regenerating and uniting mankind. . . . I have not come to propagate any particular religion. . . . Today people try to find God in religions but God is to be found not in religion but in your own mind (heart). It is only when the mind is controlled and purified that God can be recognized."

Another great Indian saint, Sri Aurobindo said, "Sanathana Dharma (the ancient wisdom; the eternal path) is the eternal law of the Divine Consciousness." In fact, Jawaharlal Nehru maintained in his life that India has no religion as such, no faith founded by a higher being or prophet. Yet, Indians are probably the most god loving people in the world, with a deeply rooted faith in the Divine or in a Divine principle. It is almost unthinkable for an Indian to begin his day without first saying a quiet prayer to God.

As Baba once said, "The truck driver folds his hands before the steering wheel before he starts his truck, the potter invokes the Divine in his wheel, the poet in his pen, and the musician in his instrument before these are made use of." Indeed this is the general attitude in a country where true genius is its spirituality.

"Some have the absurd idea," Baba said in a discourse, "that Sathya Sai Educational Institutions are religious institutions." In fact, the curricula in these institutions is permeated with Baba's teaching of universal human values, not with religious dogma. It is not religious doctrines that Baba emphasizes in his teachings. He is not trying to force any belief down anyone's throat. People are left entirely free to accept or not accept his teachings. "If you waste this chance of saving yourselves," Baba once said, "it is your own fault."

In my experience, once you have had a taste of what it is all about — to find your own true identity or divinity — it is impossible to deny his teachings. On innumerable occasions, Baba has, through his writings and discourses, emphasized the essential divinity that is inherent in every being. The common thread running through all his teachings is the call for us to realize our fundamental divinity.

Swami Vivekananda declared that, "Man is essentially divine," and Sri Aurobindo wrote in *The Life Divine*, "If it be true that Spirit is involved in Matter and apparent Nature is secret God, then the manifestation of the divine in himself [man] and the realisation of God within and without are the highest and most legitimate aim possible to man upon earth."[23]

---

[23]Sri Aurobindo, *The Life Divine* (Wilmot, WI: Lotus Light Publications, 1990), p. 4.

The
High Commissioner

In 1989, India's newly appointed High Commissioner to the United Kingdom, Sri M. K. Rasgotra, was guest speaker at a function in the Mandir at Puttaparthi. I consider myself fortunate to have been part of the capacity audience of staff, students, and devotees assembled on that day. In Swami's presence, he was introduced by Professor Saraf, Chancellor of the Sri Sathya Sai Institute of Higher Learning, as a former Ambassador to France and a former Foreign Secretary in the Indian Government.

Sri Rasgotra reminded me in many respects of the late J. Krishnamurti. He had the same distinguished appearance, the same natural ease and humbleness, and the same noblesse of heart shone through his words. Perhaps the greater people are, the more natural and humble they seem.

Sri Rasgotra told the audience, "When I first wanted to meet Baba I went to Bangalore, from there I went to Whitefield. But he was not there, so I went to Puttaparthi. But he was not there either. Finally I went on to Anantapur and I met him there. I was received in a manner that no king, prince, or head of state could have received me, and I have been received by many of them. Fifteen years, two weeks and one day have elapsed since that day. Baba asked me then, 'Why have you come?' I told Baba, 'I am going to London as Deputy High Commissioner.' 'No, High Commissioner,' Baba corrected me. 'No, Deputy High Commissioner,' I repeated. Baba corrected me again! I again contradicted Him. Three times we went on like this. 'Oh, well maybe He doesn't know the difference,' I said to myself at last, and gave up." Needless to say, Baba was right, and Sri Rasgotra subsequently was promoted to the position of High Commissioner. "How stupid can one be?" Sri Rasgotra added, laughing as he referred to the incident.

Speaking about his first appointment as Deputy Commissioner, Sri Rasgotra continued, "Baba said there would be many problems and many difficulties. 'What shall I do?' I asked. 'You do your best and I will do the rest and the result will be satisfactory,' Baba answered. So I went to London and there were indeed many problems and difficulties, but there were also many opportunities and the result was satisfactory." He said, "What have I learned since I first came to Swami fifteen years ago, in 1972? It can be described in one word—surrender. Surrender is the path of love, the path of beauty and the path of action. All your actions merge into His actions. All your thoughts unite with His thoughts. Divinity is supposed to be airy stuff and not the province of politicians and businessmen. And yet here they come, all of them—heads of state, ministers, high government officials and top executives. All kneel down at the Feet of Baba."

Sri Rasgotra went on to say that India's role in the world is not the role of a great power. "India's role is that of a teacher and a healer and this role began in Puttaparthi. It is the healing of a sick humanity and a fractured human mind. The understanding in the outside world is not yet what it should be, but it is growing and will gradually become universal. Humanity will come to live in peace and harmony. There is, however, one word in Baba's teaching I want to say something about. It is love. The love we all talk about. Human love is a very, very limited concept of love. There is only one true concept of love and that is the Lord's love for His creation. This love is without the least tinge of selfishness. This love is given to His students who are the most fortunate members of humanity on earth today."

Sri Rasgotra concluded his talk with these words quoted from Baba:

> Start your day with love
> Fill your day with love
> End your day with love
> and you belong to Swami
> And that's where I am!

After he had done *padnamaskar* (touching the feet of the Divine) to Swami, and bent down outside the entrance to the Mandir and touched the ground, he hurried to a waiting car. Sri Rasgotra was on his way to London as High Commissioner.

See Divinity in Everything and Enjoy It

As Baba sees it, the transformation of our human nature, which is imperative if we are all to survive, should not be thought of as an easy job—it certainly isn't. Eventually we have to rise to higher planes of consciousness. When exposed to higher powers, the old nature changes and gradually the old and the new natures fuse into one truth, one harmony. For that to happen, self-discipline and *sadhana* (spiritual practice) are required. In this sadhana, *vairagya* (detachment: renunciation) plays a major role.

Baba elucidated on this subject during a recent talk one rainy day in July at Prasanthi Nilayam—primarily for students who were sitting in a packed mandir or outside under the verandah. Many devotees had taken shelter from the rain under the many beautiful concrete arches that border the mandir compound from where they were able to hear Baba's words through loudspeakers.

His words, in part, were: "Divya Atma Swarupas (Embodiments of the Divine atma): The world is a vast expression of God. Man is a wonderful creation. We are something so noble and so beautiful that we can be compared to the energy that created this world. However we are not proving that we are human beings. We are enjoying everything in this world, but have no gratitude toward God.

"Human beings use their energies for destructive purposes. The cause of this is ego. How much longer will it last?

When will we change? When we give our heart to another heart, that is prema, pure and unselfish love. But prema does not exist today. We are always expecting something in return. We have the form of a human being but the intellect is of the animal level.

"Renunciation is one of the most important aspects of human life. If we are not willing to renounce, the world will force us to do so. Renunciation does not mean to live alone in some isolated place. That can develop into a disease. What exactly is it then that must be renounced? Our inherent enemies have to be renounced—desire, greed, anger, jealousy, hatred and lust. Desire results in sorrow. It never ends. If we get one thing, we are ever ready to want the next. Greed is excessive desire. It is always ready to receive, never prepared to give. It increases our impurities. Anger has so much destructive power in it, it makes us almost insane.

"Jealousy is invariably accompanied by hatred for one cannot live without the other. They always take shelter within each other. Jealousy makes its appearance when we come in contact with a person who earns greater fame than we have, or has more wealth, or is more beautiful and handsome.

"It is the weakness of ordinary human beings to develop jealousy against people who excel them in terms of wealth, position, beauty, intelligence and such qualities. The moment jealousy enters into a person, all the virtues which that person has cultivated over a long time will be destroyed. Jealousy is not going to live harmlessly inside a person. It destroys all the good qualities which are within. It destroys the human nature, it strengthens the animal nature. Therefore in the very first place, everyone has to see to it that jealousy does not enter. You should enjoy the progress of others. This is true virtue.

"It cannot be emphasized too strongly that jealousy will destroy all your good qualities. You may think it will destroy others, but in fact it will destroy you, not the others. Jealousy is all pervasive in this Kali age. It is mostly on account of jealousy that people lose their peace of mind and waste their lives."

Baba ended his discourse on renunciation by saying, "Vairagya (renunciation) is not to give up everything. See Divinity in everything and then enjoy it. That is vairagya." For me, and I am sure for many other devotees, he had given a beautiful and clear explanation of an important but little understood aspect of his teachings.

Nobel Prize winner, G. Trevelyan, reflected Baba's teachings when he said that the dangers of a nuclear bomb are great, but a greater danger is the pollution of our atmosphere by our thoughts of jealousy and hatred. He said that this is a far greater danger to the whole world because this energy is now pervading the atmosphere.

And on the subject of lust, which Baba did not go into detail about in his speech, the renowned holy man, Paramahansa Yogananda, said that women should not be treated as objects of lust, but can be looked upon as incarnations of the Mother Divine. A home is made gracious by the presence of the Divine Mother in the form of a human mother.

It is perhaps also worth mentioning that Baba does not encourage women to take a job outside the home — as it has a tendency to undermine family life when children are left in the care of others. Divorce and frigidity in the home are the consequence, and the result is unhappy relationships and uncertainty for parents and for children, who suffer and become rootless and neglected. Baba looks upon those women who live a spiritual life as "the backbone of the nation, the jewel of the home."

Swami Hariharananda, a great man of God who is a Kriya Yoga Master, once said that people are in the midst of the greatest crisis in history because science has been placing more and more power in the hands of people who have turned the world into a place full of explosives. People live a potential yet barren life while they are frantically searching for meaning and security while the solution lies in a spiritual revolution that would embrace the whole world.

That is the only thing Baba insists on—that we change radically and fundamentally—for it will bring about the revolution he aims at—a better world. It is only through a complete change of heart in the individual that there can come about a change in society, and as a result, peace in the world. Baba helps us to see ourselves as we really are, for it is in the act of seeing with absolute clarity that the inward revolution takes place. Baba's hopes for the future rest primarily with the younger generation, and his great call is to incorporate human values in the educational systems of our time. It is not religion but character building, or dharma, that is the essence of Baba's teachings.

The
Salient Point

The salient point in Baba's teachings is his statement that he is God—something that many Westerners cannot accept. Most devotees accept that Baba is a Divine Personality, because he has proved this abundantly, but not God! The first fact to be clear about on this issue is that Baba's teaching is *Vedanta* (goal of the Vedas; liberation). He himself is Vedanta in action.

Sri Aurobindo wrote in *Life Divine*: "In truth, the difficulty thus sharply presented arises only if we assume the existence of an extracosmic personal God, not Himself the universe, one who has created good and evil, pain and suffering for His creatures, but Himself stands above and unaffected by them, watching . . . a suffering and struggling world driven . . . by an inexorable law, unhelped by Him or inefficiently helped, then not God, not omnipotent, not all-good and all-loving."[24]

According to the Vedas, which are supposed to be the highest authority in spiritual matters, consciousness consists of many planes. This is now even acknowledged by modern science. The highest Divine plane is omnipotent, omnipresent, and omniscient. According to Sri Aurobindo, this stage of consciousness is "beyond any mental definition or descrip-

24Sri Aurobindo, *Life Divine* (Wilmot, WI: Lotus Light, 1990), p. 94.

tion, positive or negative, for none of the minds' definitions can express it."[25]

Swami Hariharananda wrote that the spiritual truth propounded by the Vedas is not a product of speculation but is a result of centuries of patient research—the Vedas have discovered the ultimate truth. The ancient Vedic rishis knew the highest plane of consciousness because they lived in it, as does the Avatar, or Godman of today. His manifestation proves to the world that it does exist. It is rare indeed to come in contact with such a Godman. Our parents give us physical birth, but the Divine Master gives us spiritual birth, which is infinitely more precious for it leads to ultimate freedom. If we are faithful to his words, gradually it will dawn on our human minds that we are being guided by the Divine.

Baba is the Divine Consciousness manifest in a human body and therefore in India—the motherland of the Vedas—he is widely considered to be God. It is perfectly logical when seen in the context of the Vedantic or Hindu definition of the word. Baba is the Divine Consciousness that simultaneously sees all and knows all with boundless, inexhaustible love, not just here and there, but everywhere. I remember hearing a student once say, "Once we love Swami everything becomes easy," and this is true whether we are near him or far away. Sometimes devotees living far away are "closer" to Baba than those living in his physical presence.

Even if there is a seemingly insurmountable barrier between our human consciousness and the Divine Consciousness, which is beyond any of the mind's descriptions, there remains a point of contact between them just as there is a point of contact between the wave and the ocean. The wave cannot measure the immensity of the ocean, but when the wave merges into the ocean, it becomes one with the ocean's

---

[25]The Vedas is the name used to refer to India's ancient sacred literature, which dates back before the Christian period and is written in Sanskrit. This literature is not considered a human work but sacred knowledge. Vedanta is the philosophy based on the Vedas. It is sometimes also referred to as Neo-Vedanta.

strength and vastness. When the little human mind surrenders to the Divine Mind, it loses nothing but its limitation and deformity. At the same time, the human mind changes its nature and assumes the nature of the greater truth to which it surrenders. Unfortunately, the Western mind seems so overgrown with weeds and thistles, so arrogant and self-centered, that it cannot fathom this simple truth. The Divine has descended into matter, to lead us toward this truth.

Baba says, "To experience the all-pervading Consciousness is to experience God." Vedanta is not a high-flown philosophy that no one can understand; the teaching in Sri Sathya Sai Colleges is based on Vedanta, or higher learning, therefore they are called Sri Sathya Sai Institutes of Higher Learning. Baba has explained to his students, in his own charming words, what Vedanta is: "He who is in you and in me is Vishnu, the Omnipresent, the One. This is the supreme Truth. Then, why do we not pardon others when they do harm to us? Why can we not put up with our pain without hating the people who caused it? The Self (Atma) in every person and everything is one—the same. Each one in this wide world is a unit of the Self, a bead strung on the same thread. This is the secret that is identified and revealed in the Vedanta. Vedanta advises us to discard differential vision and cultivate the unifying vision of love. The five elements are involved in loving mutuality.

"As smoke envelops fire, desire envelops awareness of truth. When one has no desires one's intellect is clear and one's discrimination is sharp—*atmajnana viheenaa moodhaah*—says the Vedanta. Human beings long to own all things that promise to give joy, and are entrapped by them. Too much desire tarnishes the mind—this is the warning administered by Vedanta.

"In human beings we can also discern certain beasts and birds. How does a cow behave? When you wave a bunch of grass, it runs toward you, when you wave a stick, it runs away from you. Man, too, acts similarly. If we see some benefit, we come to God; if no benefit accrues, we give up worship. Vedanta opens the eyes of such ignorant persons.

"Within life, death exists; within love, there dwells hatred; night is encased by day; old age hides within youth. Everything has inevitably to confront its opposite! Iron is hard and black; when heated it turns soft and red. So, too, through Vedanta, the human mind turns luminous and full of charm.

"Vedanta is a treasure we all need. It is the seed from which awareness of Divinity sprouts; indeed it is the very basis of self-knowledge. Does not Vedanta show the paths to liberation, of involvement and of withdrawal with the sole purpose of saving mankind? Vedanta teaches the very basis of all knowledge, that which when known, can give us the knowledge of everything—namely the knowledge of the supreme soul, the Paramatma. Human beings have forgotten Reality; Vedanta brings it back to memory. God is Supreme Consciousness. When the individual consciousness is merged in the Supreme Consciousness, unbounded bliss is the reward.

"Human beings delude themselves, mistaking the momentary as the momentous; we barter the precious gem, holy life, for a piece of charcoal and close our mortal career. Vedanta, the Higher Learning warns *anithyam asukham lokam, imam praapya, bhajaswa maam* (having reached this transient, travail-full world, worship me). However, what do we find? Everyone, young and old, is sunk in selfishness. Consideration for others is confined to words only. It is absent in action.

"The awareness of one's Divinity cannot be won by book learning, it has to be earned through the culture of the mind. This culture is now very rare. Many are in the grip of greed, though they have wealth, they do not spend it for the good of others. Their plight is like the frog, trapped in the cobra's mouth, jutting out its tongue to catch a passing fly!

Vedanta teaches such unfortunate ones to surrender to the will of God and be at peace.

"Spirituality must transform the bad into good people. Otherwise it cannot be Vedanta—or Higher Learning. This teaching has to abolish violence, selfishness, hatred, envy and pride from man's mind. It guides us to acquire expansive hearts, detached attitudes, contented minds, and loving personalities.

"All are students enrolled in the University that the eternal universe is. The blacksmith, the potter, the carpenter, the mendicant, the farmer, the artisan, the trader, the poorest of the poor and the richest among the rich, are all learning lessons in this university as students in various classes at various levels.

"Students of today must act. They must realize that the moral strength in them is being sapped by Western culture and education. Western culture is the culture of the metropolis, where the multiplication of individual desires has led human beings to misery and unhappiness. The present education system does little for enrichment and spiritual unfoldment. It has merely brought society to the brink of disaster. We therefore require today students with broad minds, people of action capable of selfless service. Simple living and high thinking should be the ideal, not high living and low thinking, which seems to be the maxim of modern education.

"Human life is comparable to a tree and kinsmen of the individual to its branches. On these branches the flowers of his thoughts and feelings blossom. These flowers gradually develop into fruits of good qualities and virtues. The nectarine juice present in these fruits is character. Without roots and fruits, a tree is mere firewood. Self-confidence is the root of the tree of life and character is its fruit."

This is a magnificent exposition of the importance, purpose, and value of the Vedanta, and we are fortunate, indeed, to have it from Baba himself.

Surrender

What does "surrender" mean? To whom do we surrender? For many people this aspect of Baba's teaching, or any spiritual teaching, is difficult to understand. The word itself can be misleading, but it is the best word we have to describe the process.

Surrender in spiritual life means to give ourselves to the Divine, but it also means to find ourselves. But how can we find something we hardly know? First, we must have a "taste" of surrender, and that comes from reading, and above all, from living the Divine's powerful words. It has been said that perfect self-giving is perfect self-finding. In this context, the self is not the ego; in fact to find the self we must let go of the ego. When we become aware that beyond the ego there is something worth seeking, we are on our way toward overcoming the ego.

All saints, and every avatar, tell us that the ego has to go if we want to let go of the false and find the truth. Surrender really means giving up the ego, which is false. But instead of going through a grim struggle to overcome the ego, we can offer it to the Divine. In doing this we find an inner warmth—a beauty—and a creative life. It is a sweet way of bidding the ego farewell.

While actually writing this book in the *mandap* at Whitefield, I experienced another of Baba's charming leelas. The 'mandap' is an open area just inside the gate at Whitefield where Baba gives darshan. It is protected from the weather by a circular cast iron roof built around the trunk of a huge pipal tree (the sacred fig tree in India) that towers overhead, spreading its foliage over the entire site. The diameter of the covered circle is about fifty meters. At the base of the tree is a raised concrete platform that features a statue of Krishna playing his *murali* (flute).

I was sitting in line writing while waiting for Baba to come out and give darshan. He was still in the *mandir* (temple), perhaps a hundred fifty meters away, when I saw something that looked like a small white feather come whirling through the air. It landed on my writing pad. I picked it up. It was a white jasmine. Jasmine is the fragrance most often associated with Baba's presence, and I knew instantly it was Baba's leela, a token of his grace and an encouragement, I felt, to go on. I picked up the thread of my writing again with the jasmine in my hand and its lovely perfume in my nose.

As we learn and experience for ourselves Baba's Christ-like powers, surrender—or the will to surrender—comes almost naturally. How can we not give ourselves to someone whose divinity shines through every pore of his being? He has his own way of doing things, but if he sees someone in need, even an animal, he is there with his soothing balm.

An example is the following story from a lady who follows Baba. She said: "Almost each day of my stay at Prasanthi Nilayam I walked through the village, past the schools, past the new planetarium to the large plot of tropical land that is Sai Gita's home. Often I would stop at one of the many small fruit and vegetable stands along the roadside and pick out five or six ripe bananas to take to the elephant. Usually the *mahout* (keeper) who took care of Gita allowed me to feed her and stroke her trunk.

"One morning, as was my practice, I waved at the keeper and held up my gift of bananas. Holding up his hand in returned recognition, he walked toward the entrance. Taking the fruit from my hand he said, 'I will not have you feed these to Gita today.' I responded quickly, 'Is she sick?' 'No, no,' came his reply, 'Swami may stop and feed her these bananas today.'

"I thought to myself, I have been here almost every day and Swami has never stopped to feed her. Why, sometimes he hasn't even looked her way. This man must be dreaming. I finally decided the keeper was going to eat the bananas himself. No sooner had this thought gone through my mind than a student, neatly dressed in fresh white trousers with matching shirt, galloped up to the gateway and shouted to the elephant keeper that Swami was indeed on his way.

"Wiping Gita's trunk and straightening her bell, the keeper walked with Sai Gita to the entrance. He opened the gate and she stepped out onto the sand to wait in anticipation for Swami. She bowed low and trumpeted loudly as his red car came to a stop in front of her. The door opened and Swami stepped out. Walking several steps toward Gita, he reached out and put his arms around her trunk and gave her a hug. Gita closed her eyes in ecstasy. Swami then took the bananas and fed them one by one to Gita, stroking her trunk as she ate.

"I was breathless. How had the keeper known Swami would stop there that day? Nudging me gently, the keeper pointed to the camera that hung forgotten around my neck, then to Swami, reminding me of the opportunity to take pictures. What went on between God and beast that day was inexpressible. The love that passed between them was glorious. As Swami's car vanished down the narrow road, I turned to the keeper in near hysteria. 'How did you know Swami would stop and feed Gita today?' I asked, almost screaming.

"Softly, the man replied, 'I didn't know. What I did know was that Gita needed to be close to Swami. She had been waiting for a long time. God gives each of us what we need, not just to humans, but to each species of creation. Every being is in his ever-knowing hands.' "

I have also seen several examples of Gita's "surrender" to and love for Swami. When Swami leaves for a visit to White-field she is taken down to the roadside by two keepers and as he passes she lifts her trunk and trumpets loudly while tears run down her huge cheeks. The love expressed by animals can be more psychic than that of human beings. What humans call love is often merely an exchange of mutual satis-faction and entertainment.

Without love there can be no surrender. They go together. Surrender in the yogic sense takes time. But even the first attempts at surrender give such a wonderful inner calm and sense of serenity, it is hard to imagine having been able to live without it. It is the act of the soul giving itself that makes a fusion with the Divine possible. Surrender is thus a very important aspect of Baba's teachings. The soul that gives itself to the Divine does not do so in vain. Expecting nothing, it receives all.

Sanathana Dharma

Although Baba's teachings are not a religion in the accepted sense of the word — meaning a mass of theological dogmas — his teachings are deeply religious. Baba has said, "a religious (sacred) mind is a mind that is capable of finding out the truth." His teachings are based on *Sanathana Dharma*, which means the eternal Truth of the Divine Consciousness, and therefore Baba's teachings embrace all religions.

Baba says, "All religions are derived from a person, a prophet who is adored as the ideal. Islam has Muhammad, Christianity has Jesus, Buddhism has the Buddha. But Sanathana Dharma is not derived from or through a person. It unites all faiths through its innate strength."

The Sri Sathya Sai emblem, Sarva Dharma, is a symbol of Sanathana Dharma with the AUM symbol at the top. Sarva means all comprehensive, universal, and the essence of Dharma is love. The emblem also represents the essential unity of all religions, emphasizing that there is only one God.

Baba says, "Where there is love, there is peace. Where there is peace, there is divinity, and where there is divinity there is Bliss."

Sanathana Dharma does not aim at a personal salvation in some far off heaven because this world is too painful a place in which to live. It is here, and not elsewhere, that the highest godhead must be found and nothing but an entire

self-giving or surrender to the highest will bring us to the highest. Sanathana Dharma sees all life as God's mighty pulsation. All life is God.

As Baba says, "Sanathana Dharma is bound to overcome today's rampant materialism, for it harmonizes the secular and the spiritual into a single way of life. It is based on the Divine, which is the reality of the Self (our innermost being). Therefore it is not limited to one country or one individual. It is the vital air on which humanity has to live. It is welcomed by all mankind for it welcomes all mankind. The essence of all religions, the goal of all paths, is Sanathana Dharma." It is through Sanathana Dharma that we can attain the fullness of life, materially, mentally and spiritually. It is the goal to which we are led by the Avatar.

Baba has told us, "Outward religion cuts existence into two opposite categories, the holy and the profane, the spiritual and the worldly. Do not be misled by a belief in two entities — this world and the next, here and hereafter. Realize the hereafter here. This world is interwoven with the next; each is necessary to the other. There is no truth in the disparity between the secular and the spiritual, the godly and the materialistic, the heavenly and the earthly."

Baba has said, "When asked where God is, people point toward the sky or some far distant region; that is why He is not manifesting Himself. Realize that He is in you, with you, behind you, before you and all around you."

PART TWO

BABA'S LEELAS

The
Only Criterion

The Umbrella: Baba has always said that the only criterion for understanding his omnipotence and omniscience is your own experience of them. One such experience of mine occurred when I was standing on the verandah on the ladies side of the mandir at Prasanthi Nilayam. I was looking through the window at Baba who was sitting on his chair inside the temple during bhajans.

I was fascinated by his face. It was so radiant with a quality of inner beauty, so full of infinite sweetness, so powerful, so deeply calm with a pure, classical profile. How his divinity shone through that wonderful face. He turned and looked at me with a kindly smile.

While standing there I held between my feet a folded cushion, which I used to sit on during darshan. Inside the fold of the cushion was my umbrella. It was a gift my son bought for me in London, and unfortunately it had become quite a nuisance to use. The handle, designed like the handle of a walking stick and more suitable for a man, kept falling off every time I put the umbrella up. As I bent down to pick up my cushion and umbrella I saw that it now had a new, neat, small and carved lady's umbrella handle. I could hardly believe my own eyes, but there it was. Without my noticing, while I was standing there looking at Baba as he sat in his chair some fifteen meters away with the thick stone wall of the mandir between us, Baba had put a new handle on the umbrella. In his own way, he had reminded me that he is always with his devotees, and specifically, that he knew what a bother the original umbrella handle had been to me.

It was particularly special to me because at the time I used the umbrella constantly. The ashram doctor had told me to protect my face against the sun at all times to avoid the risk of any recurrence of the cancerous growth I had had on my face. When, through wear and tear, the umbrella eventually had to be discarded, I kept the handle, which is still in a drawer in my flat at Prasanthi Nilayam.

The Campstool: During one of Baba's talks in the auditorium at Prasanthi Nilayam, I was seated on a very uncomfortable campstool. After about an hour I was aching all over and couldn't even listen to what was being said. Silently I asked Baba for help.

Before I knew what was happening I was sitting on the floor—I had gone right through the seat of that stool! Baba sent me a discrete side glance while he was talking, but there was a smile playing on his lips. I was immediately given a good chair to sit on!

"I Will See": Devotees regularly communicate with Baba without using the spoken word. One day at darshan, Baba was standing in front of me pointing to the devotee seated next to me while waiting to go in for an interview. I, too, felt a need for an interview. I silently asked Baba, "Will you also give me an interview, Swami?" He answered out loud, "I will see," so everyone could hear, although no one could have known to what Baba was referring. The next day I was given an interview during which Baba sent me a meaningful look, as if to say, "See, I did give you an interview, didn't I?"

A Dose of his Shakti: At a time when I was feeling ill and running a high temperature, I asked Baba to come and see me. He came in a dream during a siesta. As Baba has said a number of times, his presence in a dream is real. It cannot be conjured up as a figment of imagination.

In my dream I saw him standing in the doorway, on his way out, as if he had been in the room for some time. He was looking at me as he stood there, but I could only see part of his face and body because the rest was hidden by the door. He didn't say anything but turned that wonderful face of his toward me as if to say, "Are you happy now, my child?" — like a mother who has come to see her sick child. "Yes, dearest Swami, I am happy now," I said, "particularly when you visit me in this way."

His visit had a soothing effect. When I got up, a feeling of life, strength, and vitality flowed through my being. Gone was the fever, and I felt refreshed, like a young girl. He had given me a dose of his *shakti* (his omniscient love).

The Tractor Driver: My friend and I were returning to Prasanthi Nilayam by taxi after a visit to Bangalore. About forty kilometers from the ashram, as darkness fell, the lights of the taxi failed. The driver was unable to fix them and to drive on in the night without lights was dangerous. Yet for the three of us to spend the night in the car, in that desolate spot, was also dangerous. What, then, were we to do? After some discussion my friend remembered she had a small flashlight in her handbag. We decided to proceed, with our brave driver using one hand to hold the flashlight out the side window of the car while he steered the car with the other hand. We proceeded at a snail's pace, knowing that at that speed it would take us until next morning to reach Prasanthi Nilayam.

We called on Swami repeatedly because our return journey had become so difficult. Suddenly the driver slammed on the brakes just before the car almost plunged headlong down a slope off the road. We were fortunate. The driver had become aware of the danger at the last possible moment.

At that point, of all things, a tractor mysteriously appeared out of the darkness. The tractor driver quite happily drove his machine behind our taxi for more than an hour, shining his powerful lights through the windows and onto the road ahead so we could travel at a reasonable speed. He went many kilometers out of his way and saw us safely back all the way to the gates of the ashram, where we arrived at about 10:00 P.M.

The ashram gatekeeper was not too pleased about our late arrival until the reason for the delay was explained to him. My friend and I, tired and dusty after our eventful trip, silently thanked Swami for his care and protection as we made our way to the sanctuary of our rooms. To me this was another of the many thousands of examples of how Baba always protects his devotees.

Vibhuti

Vibhuti is the sacred ash that Baba produces almost daily to give to someone in need. Its curative powers are well-known. Baba creates vibhuti with a simple circular wave of his hand, palm down, as if it is the most natural thing in the world. Indeed, the devotees have become so accustomed to seeing the feat regularly performed that it is easy to forget what an immense power of creation is involved in this seemingly simple act.

No wonder Baba draws such enormous crowds wherever he goes. In every respect he symbolizes all that humankind is longing for—peace, joy, and bliss—the opposite of what is found in today's world. His ashram is filled with this kind of peaceful atmosphere to such an extent that it is almost tangible, and can be felt many kilometers from Prasanthi Nilayam. Baba stands for the unity of humankind, a unity that rests in the Divine and in which he himself is the divine soul. Baba's teachings are not restricted to ideas. Often they are actual experiences. He can make you sit next to an old, toothless village woman whose worn and wrinkled face has been scorched by the sun, who has rarely had a wash, who has known starvation and many other trials, and in some strange way make your body feel all the suffering this woman has gone through. Or he can make many a devotee, perhaps particularly those who prize their intellect, go through a crucible until he or she sees that intellectual arrogance and haughtiness are a childish and hollow reaction to something infinitely greater.

The Divine consciousness is infinitely more comprehensive and complex than the human consciousness, however intelligent it may appear to be. Divinity has forces at its disposal and operates in a way that the human intellect cannot begin to fathom. As one of the great human intellects of our time, Albert Einstein once said that the most beautiful and most profound emotion anyone can experience is the sensation of the mystical — to know that what is impenetrable to us really exists, manifesting itself as the highest wisdom and the most radiant beauty which our dull faculties can comprehend — this knowledge — this feeling is at the center of true religiousness.

Without the adoration of the heart, the endeavor of the will, and the thirst of the feelings, human nature lacks the strength needed to carry through this unique opportunity to transcend itself and reach its highest nature. It is for this, then, that the avatar has come, to inspire human beings to follow this great call and to persist until that goal has been reached.

Leelas
as Lessons

A student at one of Baba's colleges, gave a talk in the Poorna-chandra Hall at Prasanthi Nilayam, and began with the familiar quotation from William Shakespeare: "Ignorance with love is better than wisdom without." He went on to describe three of Baba's leelas that he knew about personally. The first one involved himself.

"I was very fond of playing cricket. One morning when I was on my way to the cricket ground I had a strange feeling that I should not play that day. Still I went; I was too fond of the sport. On the sports ground I got yet another warning from our sports leader who said, 'Be careful about your glasses when you play.'

"I answered rather casually, 'Don't worry, I know the game and how to look after myself.' However, through a chance maneuver the ball hit the glass over my left eye. The glass splintered in many small pieces that fell outside, away from the eye, and nothing happened to my eye. I was, however, very upset. How easily could a glass splinter have gotten into my eye and made me lose the vision in that eye. I thanked Swami for saving my eye. My parents have a big photo of Swami in their drawing room. When my glasses were broken that photo fell on the floor and the glass that covered it splintered into many small pieces, but only over the left eye. The rest of the glass covering the picture remained intact."

The second leela involved a friend of the student's family. "A devotee who lived in Calcutta, a friend of ours, was a successful businessman who had many branch offices in other cities. Swami had advised him to move out of Calcutta.

"This man did not heed Swami's advice and one day a big crowd gathered outside his house with axes, knives, and bars. The police were called but it was rather hopeless. The crowd was too agitated, the police could do nothing. The devotee rushed into his puja room, knelt down at the altar, and called fervently to Swami for help. Shortly after a car drove up and the man and his family got safely out of the house and into the car. The car, however, got stuck in the crowd. It was impossible to pass through. Baba's name was incessantly called in the mind of this devotee. Soon a man arrived who appeared to be a police inspector. He cleared a way for the car through the crowd and brought the devotee and his family to the police station where they were safe. Then he vanished. Almost immediately after this the devotee flew to Bangalore with his family to thank Swami, who at that time was in Whitefield. Swami, who of course knew all about it, asked the devotee, 'Who do you think the inspector was? It was me.'"

The third of Baba's leelas took place at the ashram. "Two gentlemen came to Prasanthi Nilayam. They were new to the place and had brought a bottle of whiskey with them. After evening bhajans, when they got back to their quarters, they took out the bottle to have a glass of whiskey. They said 'Cheers, cheers,' and took a sip to enjoy the drink, but it tasted like water.

"They were furious and decided that when they got back to Bangalore they would give the liquor shopkeeper a thorough scolding for having cheated them. At darshan the next morning they were, however, greeted by Baba saying, 'Cheers, cheers.' Then they knew who had filled their whiskey bottle with water." The student concluded his description of Baba's delightful leelas by saying, "Once we love Swami, everything becomes smooth and easy."

Usually Baba's discourses are preceded by talks from his students and often they recount examples of his leelas. When this happens I take the opportunity to keep notes so the stories can be shared with others. Here are two further examples of Baba's leelas, as described by students.

One day at Kodaikanal, when Swami was surrounded by some of his students, he suddenly shouted out, "Don't shoot." The boys, quite naturally, were amazed at this uncharacteristic outburst, but as Swami offered no explanation the incident remained a mystery. A few days later, however, a telegram arrived from an army officer and Sai devotee, who was stationed in a distant area. It explained all.

The officer, feeling depressed and utterly frustrated with his life, was contemplating suicide. With that intention, he took out his service revolver, placed it to his head, and was about to pull the trigger when there was a knock on the door. He quickly hid the revolver and opened the door to find an old man standing there whom he had never seen before. As an act of politeness, the officer invited him in. The unknown old man demonstrated a remarkable knowledge of the officer's situation and background, and after a long talk, the young officer's outlook on his life was changed. He then realized who was behind the timely and lifesaving intervention. He sent the telegram to Swami, thanking him for coming to his rescue at just the right moment.

The second story involved a lady Sai devotee and her pet cat. One day she discovered that the cat had jumped onto the table in her room and eaten a cake she had put aside to enjoy at leisure. She lost her temper, seized a stick, and struck the cat. As the cat fled, a picture of Baba hanging on the wall crashed to the floor. Afraid that her attack on the cat had something to do with the surprising fall of Baba's picture, she quickly ran to find her cat. She was astonished to see that it had a streak of vibhuti running down its back. Sometime later, as she sat in the darshan line, Baba approached where she was sitting and handed her four packets of vibhuti. His only comment was, "Two packets are for the cat." Baba tells us repeatedly, "Love is my form," and that love extends not just to human beings, but to animals and the whole of creation. Love is vast and fathomless like the ocean.

Sri Sathya Sai Baba Visits His School in Ooty

Sri Sathya Sai's school for young boys, is situated on a hilly range in Ooty, the "queen" of the Indian hill stations in the Nilgiris mountains. It is a marvelous place surrounded by tall eucalyptus and other tropical trees, with a poinsettia tree full of bright red flowers at the entrance and plenty of beautiful roses. Birds chirp in the trees, and cows graze contentedly among the thick carpets of tea bushes covering the mountain slope. On the big lawn in front of the house a former fountain now supports the central piece of the Sri Sathya Sai symbol — a lotus flower on a pillar representing the unity of all religions. Everything breathes *shanti, shanti, shanti* (peace, peace, peace).

I was fortunate to be present during one of Baba's visits to the school. In preparation, a toothless old man had swept the driveway with a broom similar to the kind witches supposedly rode in medieval times. Under a huge fir tree, several hundred years old, many ladies had sought shelter from the early alpine sun on what was a lovely mid-October morning. The men were sitting cross-legged on the lawn. Everyone seemed to enjoy sitting in the exquisite surroundings and atmosphere. There was a hush of expectation.

The doors opened and Sri Sathya Sai Baba stepped out. In his gracious way he walked slowly among the devotees; a word here, a look there, a pat on the shoulder, *vibhuti* (sacred ash) produced from his palm sprinkled down into outstretched hands, but he allowed *padnamaskar* (touching of the feet) to only a few. After a full round, he walked back into the house and the doors closed behind him. But everyone had felt the impact of the darshan. All worries were gone. He had filled everyone with his light, love, and energy—so supremely sustaining.

This particular year Deepavali, the Hindu festival of light,[1] was being celebrated in a quiet way at the school although the rest of the township of Ooty was very festive for the occasion. During the festival, fireworks cracked and ladies dressed in their most elegant saris. But in the school, the boys—looking innocent and happy—gathered at Baba's feet as their Master strolled among them. He asked one small boy to stand up, and touching him gently under the chin asked, "What do you want?" With a shy smile the boy simply replied, "You."

Adult devotees were also invited into the school during Swami's visit. There was a mad scramble at the door to get in. But inside it was as if Swami had erected an umbrella of peace and bliss under which everyone was seated perfectly at ease. The boys sang bhajans to their master as he sat on a beautifully decorated *jhoola* (swing). They couldn't take their eyes off him, nor for that matter could anyone else. The interior of the school is very simple, with the original old wooden floors intact. The building is the former summer residence of the past British Governor and I imagined for a moment how many a waltz must have been danced on those floors.

Many devotees, including some from abroad, had accompanied Sri Sathya Sai Baba into the mountains. But that year one group was unable to make it. Their van met with a serious accident, and one passenger was killed and

---

[1]Deepavali is considered the day when Rama, the hero of the *Ramayama* (believed to be the very first poem in Sanskrit) reentered Ayodhya after fourteen years of exile. Sita, his queen, lit the first lamp to celebrate his return. Deepavali symbolized the victory of virtue over vice.

another seriously injured. The survivors were puzzled that they had traveled such a long way to obtain Swami's darshan and a disaster happened. In fact some were on the point of blaming the Divine for what had taken place. Had not Baba said, "I will protect my devotees like the eyelid protects the eyeball"?

Such protection is indeed extended, provided we are living his teachings and putting his words into practice. Otherwise, how can we call ourselves devotees? There are many thousands of cases, well-documented by sincere devotees, concerning Sri Sathya Sai Baba's instant protection in moments of danger. If tragic events occur, we may safely conclude that it is we ourselves who have stepped out of his protection. Those who come to Sathya Sai Baba out of mere curiosity, or those who say in effect, "I refuse to change," those who adopt the rather dangerous attitude that they are not prepared to give up bad habits, exclude themselves from any protection.

Lord Krishna in the Bhagavad Gita said, "Fixing your mind on Me you will by My grace, overcome all obstacles, but if from egoism you will not hear Me, you will perish." It is advisable for a devotee not to place him or herself in that last category for Sri Sathya Sai Baba can be fire that burns.

Before one comes to Sathya Sai Baba, it is better to be aware of what his teachings are about. The miracles are only a side issue, not at all the real essence. Moreover, for a god-man they are not miracles, but natural, as are all the other laws that are valid for the divine consciousness that Sri Sathya Sai Baba manifests. As Sri Aurobindo wrote, "There is as much difference between that consciousness and our level of consciousness as there is between that of an animal and a human being."

What is really demanded of us is a total and radical change of our attitude to life, and if we are not prepared for that, it is perhaps better not to come to Swami. If, however, we come with an open mind and heart, we receive such a bountiful harvest that when we return home we find it has opened another dimension of life for us. Few fail to feel a change in their lives after having met Sri Sathya Sai Baba.

The Marigold

Baba has no need of eyes and ears. He sees right through doors and walls, even across continents. For example, one time he gave a detailed description of a devotee's apartment in Los Angeles! And he hears our innermost thoughts even before they are spoken and answers them. We can hide nothing from Baba, not even in our minds. Whatever you think, he knows.

I had a personal experience of Baba's omniscience in my early years in the ashram. One morning after darshan, I sat cross-legged on the sand in the mandir compound. I was most alone and quite unhappy about a number of things that were affecting the life of someone very dear to me. Baba, of course, knew all about it and was inside the mandir busy with his usual schedule when all of a sudden a marigold fell down, as if from heaven itself, right next to where I was sitting. It almost fell on my sari. I immediately became aware of it because it behaved so strangely, jumping around almost as if it were a rubber ball. Obviously here was something out of the ordinary. There are no flower beds in the compound, and none close by. I got up quickly to see if someone had perhaps thrown it to me over the wall. But there was no one in sight. I knew it was Baba who, without words, wanted to comfort me and tell me not to worry, that all would be well. My despair disappeared and I no longer felt weighed down by circumstances.

On another occasion during the same year, Baba again showed his nearness. I had just arrived back at the ashram after a short visit overseas and, among other things, had with me a large bar of Toblerone, a distinctive Swiss style chocolate. I was aware that Baba never received anything from anyone, but for some reason decided to send the Toblerone to him by mail, even though I knew such things were always returned to the sender. The village post office is just across the street from the ashram, so delivery would be certain and swift.

The next day, as I sat almost alone in the mandir compound after morning darshan, I was startled by the feel of an invisible hand gently stroking my cheek. It felt just the same as if it had been a physical hand. I felt it was Baba who was thanking me in this way. He, who has all the five elements at his command, had received a bar of chocolate from a devotee. It had been given with a pure heart, and he was moved.

The
Art of
the Avatar

Compared to anything we call love in our ordinary, everyday world, Baba's *prema* (love) is an overwhelming contrast. When devotees come in contact with Baba's prema for the first time, their reactions vary. Some feel quite elevated, others seek solitude and are, long after the first contact with this tremendous power of Baba's, unable to socialize. Others cry, as did a professor I know from Copenhagen. He cried openly during his first interview. Some feel nothing. They, themselves, have closed the door. But often after a while they open the door a little to "test" the atmosphere. Finding warmth and light they are encouraged to venture out, and gradually their initial reluctance disappears and their better self emerges.

Some people have more money than others and it may make them arrogant. Wealth is said to be one of the greatest obstacles on the path to the far greater riches of the spirit. It requires great strength, honesty, and integrity to remain unattached to material wealth. The intellect, too, can also block the way. Sri Aurobindo once wrote: "For many intellectuals, so called, their intellectuality may be a stumbling block as they bind themselves with mental conceptions or stifle their psychic fire under the heavy weight of rational thought. . . . Afterward when it (the intellect) is turned into high thought it becomes, on the contrary, a great power."

Others, yet again, do not feel any humility toward the Divine and often behave in a primitive and rude way. But in all cases, Baba uses his "art of alchemy" to remove the dross that covers the small bar of pure gold, the spark of the Divine within each of us.

Today Baba's divinity is widely known all over India, and in most countries throughout the world. But in the end, it is in our own hearts that we must find him. "Prema is my *swarupa* (nature)," he says. In his soul he embraces the soul of a devotee, and with this tremendous soul power he finds his way into all hearts. We are fortunate that such a divinity as this is at work today to restore our unbalanced human race to its inherent harmony with all creation.

Baba
Sends Flowers

On one occasion, when I had not yet grasped the magnitude of Baba's divinity, I imagined that he had committed a serious blunder in the guidance he was providing for me. "No, no," I thought to myself, "I have had enough, no more." After this mental outburst, I returned to my apartment in one of the Round Houses, a series of free-standing, multi-story, circular buildings with central courtyards, that have been constructed toward the rear of the ashram. They are about a six minute walk from the mandir where Baba lives in two small rooms.

To my surprise, when I arrived I found a garland of flowers, about twenty-five inches long, hanging on the door handle. It was made of snow-white, dew-fresh jasmine, a variety that is very rare in the busy market outside the ashram walls. I thought, "Who could be so crazy as to hang these beautiful flowers on my door?" Naturally I took the garland inside and hung it over one of Baba's pictures, from where it spread its lovely fragrance throughout the room.[2] When in time the garland withered, I threw it out without thinking any more about it. A short time later, however, there was another garland hanging on my door, although this time a different variety and not quite as fresh and beautiful as the first. My Indian name is Gita, and it was as if the garland was

---

[2]Jasmine is almost a national flower in India. In fact, Sri Aurobindo described it as a "psychic" or soul flower.

saying, "Silly Gita, don't you know who sent you these flowers?" At last I understood and immediately wrote a letter to Baba to thank him. At darshan he took my letter with a smile.

Another Sign of Grace

Another sign of grace I received from Baba was during a much more serious personal situation, at a time I was staying at Whitefield. I had developed a growth under my right eye. A biopsy showed it to be a malignant cancer. An eye specialist said it must be removed at once by surgery. But I had no confidence in any doctor, Indian or Western. Into the bargain the specialist had told me it would be a difficult operation because the growth, from where it was spreading down along the nose, was also right under the tear duct. If it was unsuccessful, he said, I would have tears running down my face for the rest of my life. I tried to be brave, but I'm afraid I wasn't!

At the time Swami was in Madras, so I quickly obtained his address and sent him a cable about my difficulty. At Whitefield I live within the ashram in a simple Indian style, self-contained apartment that has no telephone. Yet that evening Swami's voice came to me as clearly as if it had been a call from Madras. Three or four times, in that infinitely soothing voice of his, he said, "Gita, don't worry. I will be with you." I felt a feeling of great relief.

The operation was to take place about a week later. The day before, I packed a few necessities and took a taxi to the hospital. The next day I was taken into the operating room in a wheelchair, where six or seven doctors and nurses were gathered. They all were perceptibly nervous. One nurse started stammering, the chief physician who was to perform the operation spoke in a loud, strained voice, and it occurred to me that I was the only calm person in the room. I refused a full anesthetic in favor of a local.

As I watched what seemed to me to be the thick, clumsy fingers of the doctor who was to perform this encroachment, I prayed fervently for Swami to take over. And he did. I felt so clearly that it was he who performed the operation that I had to exercise great self-control to prevent tears, which wouldn't have helped things at all, from flowing down my cheeks. About a week later when the stitches were removed, there was not the slightest trace of a scar, which the doctors had told me would be unavoidable.

The surgeon then showed me some medical photos before and after an identical operation for the same tumor, in the same place, that had been performed by a professor at the University of Massachusetts in the United States. The face of the patient had been completely pulled to one side and looked ugly and deformed. Yet to this day my face is a perfectly normal shape, without any scar.

It is one thing to hear about Swami's countless leelas, it is quite a different thing to experience them for yourself. As soon as Swami returned from Madras, I wrote him a letter to thank this doctor of doctors for having saved my eye, my face, and my life.

The
Supreme Parent

At one point in my life I went through a phase where I felt completely dried out—like a squeezed lemon without a drop of juice left. My work of trying to write about my experiences of Baba and his teachings appeared overwhelmingly difficult. To capture what I knew in words sometimes seemed impossible. I doubted that I would ever make it through to the end. I was so overcome, I even stopped going to darshan and bhajans. Instead I went on early morning walks in the lovely, serene countryside behind the ashram.

One morning, as I sat on a rock contemplating my situation, I caught sight of a little squirrel sitting on the roof of a small, ramshackle shed. With incredible speed and adroitness it moved its bushy tail like a baton saluting the rising sun, the first rays of which were appearing over the rocks. It looked so happy and uncomplicated as it jumped about on the roof. Each time it sat down, its tail again flashed its signal to the sun, inviting it to shine for another day on the world.

A little higher up in the rocks there appeared to be a cave where a *sadhu* (one who has devoted himself to the pursuit of truth) was living. I could clearly hear him chopping wood and now and again his head could be seen above some huge boulders in front of the cave, which was well-hidden from public gaze. The sadhu had evidently had enough of the material world, a feeling I could readily identify with given my despondent frame of mind.

Some distance away a loud, terrible squeak emanated from underneath a rock, sounding as if some animal had been caught under it. Eventually two men arrived, and bending down in front of the boulder, pushed something underneath it. Recently a big wolf had been seen roaming the countryside and I thought it might be the wolf's cub. Apparently it was not the first time the two men had brought food for the helpless creature.

When I eventually returned to the ashram I felt somewhat refreshed after my sojourn with nature. That evening I still had no inclination to go to darshan or bhajans, but Baba called me. At the very last minute I went to evening bhajans.

The omnipresent divinity knew, of course, all about the state of mind I was in. He doesn't allow a devotee to be downhearted for too long. At *Arathi*, after bhajans that evening, he sent such a cascade of peace down over my head it was all I could do to withhold my tears.

Arathi is an Indian ritual performed at the conclusion of bhajans or any other function presided over by Baba. Literally it is the worship of God with the flame of camphor, which burns completely leaving no residue. Symbolically the flame represents the burning of all desires, leaving no residue to impede merging with God. Similarly the flame of the love of God must consume the ego, leaving no trace of "I" and "mine."

There is no doubt that Baba is the supreme parent who takes more loving care of his child than does any physical parent. Life at the feet of such a parent can be very sweet. There can also be moments when the contact seems lost, as I have described, but that's just a passing cloud. Physical nearness is not a condition for establishing that contact, but having established it, everything changes. It is like going from a dark room out into the wonderful healing power of the sun.

Two Dreams

Like most devotees and spiritual aspirants, I have often puzzled over the contents of some of my dreams. Sri Aurobindo wrote that symbolic dreams and visions have value and sometimes considerable spiritual utility. I readily recall one dream in which I was visiting a house where the atmosphere was heavy and gray. The person living in it did not seem to be very happy, despite a high position in life and an interest in spiritual life. After I left the house, I had to climb a steep mountain. On my way up the mountain, a small child suddenly appeared at my side and wanted to follow me. According to Sri Aurobindo, a child usually signifies the psychic being or soul, and in the dream I saw this child as the soul of the person I had just been visiting.

After a while the child simply disappeared, unable to follow any longer because the mountain was too steep. Shortly after another child appeared, this time a sweet, quiet little boy. I was very determined not to give up however hard the climb might become at times, but as the small boy untiringly removed all obstacles in my path, the hardships of the journey were greatly alleviated. He was a beautiful soul.

Finally we both reached the summit of the mountain. From the top we could see wide expanses of a picturesque and serene landscape. Everything was bathed in a white light—but strangely, there were no shadows. The atmosphere was saturated with calmness and purity.

According to Sri Aurobindo a mountain is the symbol of the embodied consciousness based on earth but rising up toward the Divine. White light, he said, is a manifestation of pure Divine love. The first person I met on this mountaintop was a man standing in a garden pruning pink roses. He asked the little boy to go down into the valley below and get some tools for him. At this I became very upset, saying, "How can you ask such a question after we have just arrived here after a very arduous climb?" But he was adamant, and the boy went down to get the tools. The atmosphere on the summit was so peaceful that I was unable to utter any further words of anger; they stuck in my throat. Sri Aurobindo tells us that pink roses represent psychic love or surrender.

I had another vivid dream about a place at the very opposite end of physical nature—not on a beautiful mountaintop but in a filthy hole deep in the bowels of the earth. To me the hole represented the falsehood of the material world. Baba was sitting in the hole surrounded by an immense heap of garbage and dirt. It was impossible to see an end to it, it seemed as vast as the earth itself. From where Baba was sitting a long line of devotees was moving from the bottom toward the top of the heap, digging away at all the dirt and filth.

For some reason I was not taking part in the digging process, but I was horrified to see where Baba was sitting. A brilliant white light emanated from him. Our gaze met for a split second, and I can still recall the look in his eyes. It was as if his eyes were on fire, burning with a flame of intense compassion.

To me this dream symbolizes Baba's mission on Earth. As he lifts all mankind upward toward the Divine nature that is inherently theirs, he is removing all the impurities that cover the human heart—and indeed the whole planet.

Although Sri Aurobindo said symbolic dreams can have their use in spiritual life, he also said, "But naturally this is not supreme—the supreme thing is the realization, the contact, the union with the Divine. It is the greatest thing to which humanity can aspire."[3]

[3]Sri Aurobindo, *Letters on Yoga*, Vol. 2 (Pondicherry, India: Sri Aurobindo Ashram Trust, 1970), p. 936.

A Drop of Baba's Divinity

Every day one experiences a new aspect of Baba's divinity and his infinite sweetness. I remember one particular evening at Puttaparthi, after bhajans, when I felt I had experienced a taste of Baba's divinity that filled me with an inexpressible sweetness. It was as if the divine had put just one drop of his sweetness into me. I went and stood outside the mandir compound wall under an Ashok tree, quite a distance from the window of Baba's room but in front of it, silently telling my Lord, "How infinitely sweet you are."

It was in winter, when it gets dark early, and suddenly a flash of light appeared on the wall right next to his window. It vanished abruptly and then came back again three times. It could not have come from a torch because of the distance involved and because the shape of the light was oblong, quite unlike the beam thrown by a torch. In any case, no one in the ashram would presume to shine a torchlight near Baba's window. I knew who had caused the light to flash on the wall — Baba had heard my prayer of thanksgiving and, because it came from the depths of my heart, he had responded.

Sincerity is the key that opens the door to the divine's heart, a heart that is as big as the universe. It is not easy to win Baba's grace, as he himself says. One has to work hard to obtain it and above all one has to be SINCERE. Lip service won't do. He takes no notice of it.

The White Cobra

One evening, when I was sitting on a rock behind the ashram enjoying the supreme peace Baba had filled me with during Arathi, a strange phenomenon appeared on the western horizon—a light shining way above the ground. As I watched, the light grew and grew until it looked like the flame of a huge candle hanging in the air. It was vibrating as if alive, just like the flame of a real candle and had the same yellowish-orange color. I couldn't believe my own eyes and climbed on and off my rock several times to see if it made any difference, but it was still there. Fascinated by this magnificent and powerful light burning in the night sky, I stayed sitting quietly on my rock for quite some time in the stillness of the evening.

It was not the first time I had seen such a light. Once I saw it while sitting in the twilight on the terrace of a hotel in Kodaikanal, trying to do *tapa* (repetition of the Divine's name). The light would suddenly jump out of a hill in the distance and come and go three times. It was as if Swami was quickly repeating, "yes, yes, yes," three times, which is a characteristic of his. While living in the Sri Aurobindo ashram I also had several experiences of seeing the symbols of Sri Aurobindo and the Mother in a diamond white light in the dark evening sky over Pondicherry.

According to Sri Aurobindo, in his book *More Lights on Yoga*, "The frequent seeing of lights . . . is usually a sign that the seer is not limited by his outward surface or waking consciousness but has a latent capacity for entering into the experiences of the inner consciousness of which most people are unaware but which open by the practice of Yoga. By this opening one becomes aware of subtle planes of experience and worlds of existence other than the material. For the spiritual life a still further opening is required into an inmost consciousness by which one becomes aware of the Self and Spirit, the Eternal, and the Divine."[4]

A few days after the incident at Prasanthi Nilayam, I went back to the same place and sat on the same rock to look again for the light, but it didn't appear. Instead a gentleman approached me and said, "Madam, please don't sit here after it has become dark. There are cobras here." He suggested that I finish my meditation and return to the ashram, which I did, although having never seen any cobras in the area I didn't really believe in his warning.

A few months later, when the season had changed and I was enjoying a stroll on a light summer evening, I suddenly came across a "white" cobra. Its skin was actually light gray but its ornamentation was grayish-white, giving the overall impression of a white cobra. The beautiful creature was obviously well aware of my approach because it had its hood raised. At the sight of it I stood absolutely rooted to the spot. Not even an eyelash flickered. But the cobra didn't seem to have any hostile intentions and in fact looked quite peaceful as it glided noiselessly away, with its hood still raised. The cobra is recognized as one of Shiva's symbols and Baba is considered to manifest the great Shiva powers. Meeting a cobra in his ashram is regarded as an auspicious sign. I must admit I didn't think of that during my encounter with the poisonous snake, but I didn't feel any fear.

---

[4]Sri Aurobindo, *More Lights on Yoga* (Pondicherry, India: Sri Aurobindo Ashram Trust, 1983), p. 73.

"Swami,
Where Are You?"

There are times when Baba can seem so severe that your heart cries out, "Swami, where are you?" It is then that you must look inside yourself to discover the cause of his unflinching sternness. You will always find a hidden corner of your being—an obscure, dark spot and you can then bring his light down upon it.

You also begin to understand that his severity is an expression of his love. He wants you to live in his image, and in that image there can be no flaws. That insight re-establishes the intimacy of the relationship between the divinity and the *sadhaka* (a person aspiring to make spiritual progress), and it is confirmed by two dark eyes looking at you with such compassion, shining like two evening stars. When the divine looks so gently into your very soul like that, you know what it is to love. You are transported into another world where anger and other negative feelings quite simply don't exist. The fear that stalks the world today has no place there either, nor has the feeling of boredom that plagues so many people. The mind is expanded. Everything becomes so simple and natural. There is no speculation about what to do or not do. There is spontaneous sympathy with everything. A feeling of calmness and joy comes from the awareness that the Divine is in you.

You begin to sense the truth of Baba's words: "There is nothing I do not see, nowhere I do not know the way, no problem that I cannot solve. I am the totality, all of it." You become conscious of the fact that you are part of that totality.

Political Unrest

During a time when there was political unrest in the state of Andhra Pradesh, where Baba's ashram is situated, Baba came to my rescue once again. A senior government official and several other people had been killed in Anantapur, a nearby town, and as a result there was no traffic on the roads. Bus and train services had been suspended. Mail and telegraphic services were also not functioning. Even in the village of Puttaparthi the atmosphere was tense, and a curfew was imposed in the ashram. For the first time, I saw the big iron gates at the ashram's two main entrances closed.

For me personally, the curfew created a problem. Before the trouble began and the curfew was imposed, I had arranged an overseas visit, which meant I had to reach Bangalore airport, about a hundred and eighty kilometers south of the ashram, to begin my journey. I was bound for Copenhagen to meet my son, who would be flying in from New York. We were able to see each other only rarely those days and as all flights from India were booked months ahead, I didn't want to relinquish my opportunity.

The evening before my scheduled departure, I wandered restlessly around the ashram, praying to Swami for help. Then I saw a man run forward toward a big bus parked in the ashram grounds. The driver was standing nearby so I asked him if, by any chance, he was going to Bangalore, and if so, could I go with him.

"I am leaving for Bangalore at midnight," he said, "and you can come with me but it must be on your own responsibility." I immediately accepted. Some friends who were present protested that "I was mad" to attempt the journey under the circumstances. One devotee, in no uncertain terms, tried to persuade the driver not to take me on board. But I was quite determined to go.

At midnight I boarded the bus with my luggage, the twin iron gates of the ashram swung open, and the fifty-seat bus drove out into the pitch-black night with just one passenger. I went to the back of the bus and lay down on the wide rear seat so I could not be seen, particularly when we passed through villages and towns. We were stopped several times on the journey, as officials wrenched open the door to inquire roughly whether there were any passengers. The driver always answered no, and we were allowed to drive on. Every time the bus hit a hole in the road its old-fashioned springs and nonexistent shock absorbers sent me flying in the air, but somehow I managed to land back on the seat again.

Driving at night in India can be hazardous at the best of times, and Swami has warned devotees against it. More than once passengers on their way from Prasanthi Nilayam back to Bangalore have been robbed of their passports and money. Usually robbers place a tree trunk or boulder across the road and hide behind bushes or rocks waiting for a car to stop. They are quick to assault anyone who resists their demands. But during that bus trip there was never a shadow of doubt or fear in my mind. Swami has said, "Why fear when I am here?" It didn't occur to me to be afraid.

About 6 A.M. in the morning the bus rolled into Bangalore where conditions were fairly normal, although road traffic was heavy and congested. It was impossible to get either a taxi or a motorized rickshaw. At one point, as we stopped at a red traffic light, two dispirited looking Westerners asked the driver for a lift. But he refused to let them on the bus. Shortly after I paid the driver the normal fare and got off my "personal" bus. The driver and I parted with a smile after our arduous night.

Several hours later as I sat in Bangalore airport awaiting the call to board my aircraft, I was approached by two Danish men. "Was it you," they asked, "on that big bus this morning that refused to give us a ride?"

Baba had again demonstrated how he always protects his devotees, and in this case I was able to go on and enjoy a lovely holiday by the sea in Denmark with my son. There are as many examples of Baba extending care and protection as there are hairs on his head.

The Indian Monsoon

I awoke with a start one night in my apartment at Whitefield to find water pouring down on my head. The monsoon had begun and my roof was obviously leaking. In the morning I went immediately to see the landlord in charge. He promised to seal the roof as soon as the rain stopped, but he could do nothing while the rain continued.

I had to go to Bangalore that day, about twenty-five kilometers from Whitefield, and as I left it was still raining as though the floodgates of heaven had opened. The road to Bangalore was almost flooded. Hundreds of the very poor who live in small, primitive huts along the roadside, had already seen their homes and possessions washed away. The force of the storm had uprooted trees and broken them in two like matchsticks.

Unlike in the West, there is little, if any, public or government assistance when such disasters occur in India. To see impoverished people suddenly made homeless in such circumstances, moving along the road like a herd of cattle with nothing but a staff and a cloth bundle over their shoulders containing everything they own, is a shattering experience. Virtually overnight they have nowhere to live, not a rupee in their pockets, no food, in fact nothing at all. I have seen many similar scenes in Pondicherry and elsewhere, but the sight of these dispossessed, tired, and dejected people always shakes me to the core.

Late that afternoon I returned by bus from Bangalore, got off at the stop outside the ashram, and made my way back to my apartment, walking alongside the wall that forms the southern boundary of the grounds. On both sides of the wall are big trees that are always full of monkeys. Ahead of me walked a woman and her small daughter. Suddenly one of the monkeys sprang on the woman and snatched a parcel from her hands. She screamed in shock and anger. Although both mother and daughter rushed after the monkey, it was quickly in the safety of the tree tops with its booty. Indian monkeys can be incredibly cheeky and daring, and I made sure I had a firm grip on my own parcels as I passed by.

The rain was still pouring down monotonously and as I waded through mud and water back to my apartment, I imagined what its interior must now look like. I considered asking the ashram to give me shelter in the guest house for the night. But when I opened the door and went inside there was not a drop of water to be seen. Everything was completely dry!

That morning the landlord had told me the concrete roof of the building had cracked and he could do nothing until the weather changed, but clearly something had happened during the day while the monsoon rains continued unabated. As far as I was concerned, there was only one who could possibly have prevented my apartment from being awashed.

It had been a remarkable day during which I had seen many people suffer misfortune in a variety of ways, yet in the midst of it all my own small problem had been solved. To me it was further proof of the loving care and attention Swami unfailingly extends to his devotees.

There are countless examples of Baba intervening to help those who are prepared to follow and live his teachings in their daily lives. A good illustration is the following story, told by a student at the Sathya Sai College: "I was standing on the balcony of my parent's apartment, and as I leaned on the banister it broke and I fell toward the ground below.

"As I whirled through the air, the thought flashed through my mind that all my bones would be broken when I landed. Suddenly, however, I felt myself seized by two hands, held in an upright position, and gently put down on the ground."

Another student at the same college told of the following experience: "My father and his two friends had gone out for a walk with Swami. Swami bent down and picked up a stone from the ground, saying to my father, 'Open the mouth.' But my father refused to do so as he thought Swami would put the stone in his mouth. The two friends, however, accepted the same invitation from Swami and found the stone was changed into a piece of sugar candy in their mouths. When my father saw this he also wanted a piece of sugar candy, but it was too late."

The incident should help remind us that it would be very unfortunate if we are too late accepting and following Swami's teachings.

"See, I Also Have a Kitchen in My Hand"

It has been said that Baba is the greatest challenge for human-kind, but he is also its greatest chance. The physical challenge begins in earnest when devotees first come to the ashram at Puttaparthi. Many thousands of people now flock to Baba, and on festivals and other special occasions they must learn to share vast accommodation halls with hundreds of strangers. Or they share tiny apartments, hardly any bigger in total than one average Western-style room, with three or four others. It can be quite a strain for Westerners. The amenities are basic, a bare cement floor and bathroom facilities that can be nothing more than a tap in the wall and a "squat" toilet, which to Western eyes looks like little more than a hole in the floor. Some accommodation halls now have Western-style showers and toilets and the more recently constructed Round Houses—circular buildings with a common interior courtyard—have larger rooms and "Western" bathrooms. Necessities like mattresses, camp beds and mosquito nets must be bought or hired in the village. Vegetarian meals, costing almost nothing by Western standards, are available in several community dining rooms. Activities at the ashram begin at about 5:00 A.M. in the morning and a "lights out" rule applies at 9:00 P.M. A number of devotees are fortunate enough to be full-time residents of the ashram, and I am lucky to have my own Round House apartment, which is a little piece of Denmark in India.

It is really on the psychological front that Baba is the greatest challenge. He has been known to refer to the ashram as his "Sai-chiatric" hospital. He certainly rubs the rough edges off the personalities of those who come to visit him. It can be tough, but there are few who do not change for the better after a trip to "the workshop," as it is commonly called among devotees.

Many are keen to secure an interview with Baba and the experience can be a powerful force for change in a person's life. It is not so much what Baba says, but the effect he has on those who sit at his feet. In a sense, Baba is the "super editor" of our minds, he changes certain elements in it and eliminates others to always achieve a meaningful result. At times, he has filled my mind with such bliss I have felt as if, for a moment, I have reached the zenith of heaven.

And always there are his charming leelas and plays on words. He told one German lady during an interview, "I am the dance master, but only I know the agony of teaching you the rhythm." Perhaps it is because we are too lazy to take and act on his teachings. One simple piece of advice people are often given is *A, B, C* — always be careful. It's certainly worth following in everyday life.

Sometimes Baba will materialize a watch out of thin air, with a circular wave of his hand, and present it to a devotee reminding him that the watch stands for WATCH your ACTIONS, THOUGHTS, CHARACTER and HEART.

I remember once during an interview Baba held up the palm of his hand and asked me to cup both of my hands under his. Suddenly Indian cookies started flowing from his palm. They were hot, as if taken straight from the oven. He then asked that they be distributed. There were just enough for everyone in the room. After we had eaten our delicious cookies, our hands were a little greasy, but Baba's hand was completely clean. He held up his palm and said with a twinkle in his eye, "See, I also have a kitchen in my hand."

The
Last Meal
of a Deer

Swami's love of animals is well-known and documented. This incident that took place at "Brindavan," Whitefield, is a further example of the rapport that he has—even with creatures that are regarded as timid and fearful of people.

Baba keeps a number of animals in the private temple compound at Whitefield, including deer, rabbits, and a variety of birds that he regularly visits and feeds when he is in residence. One particular deer had developed a special love for Swami and always ran straight toward him whenever he appeared.

It is usual for Swami to retire to his personal rooms in the temple building after lunch each day, from which he rarely emerges until shortly before evening darshan at about 4:30 P.M. His rooms at Whitefield, incidentally, are comfortably carpeted and furnished, a ceiling fan is set in a finely carved frame, and the entrance is marked by beautifully carved doors.

On this particular day, however, devotees saw the unusual sight of Swami descending the stairs of his house in the late afternoon carrying an apple and a banana. To their surprise he went out to feed the deer. The deer that seemed to especially feel Baba's divinity came running toward him. According to a *Seva Dal* (volunteer service worker) who accompanied Baba, there was a heartbreaking expression of sorrow in the animal's eyes. The small deer ate the apple and banana from Swami's hand while two clear tears trickled down its face. Just half-an-hour later the soul of the deer left its mortal frame.

PART THREE

THE GODHEAD OF PARTHI

Kodaikanal

The summer of 1988, after a new bhajan hall had been constructed adjacent the Kodaikanal residence, Baba decided to
spend a major part of the hot season there. Sitting at his feet in
the new hall did make darshan and bhajans a more intimate
experience, and served as an added help to self-development
and self-discovery. But outside, the scene of "booked seats"
was the same as usual! From morning to evening darshan, and
sometimes overnight, throughout Baba's entire three week
stay, there was a long row of "reserved" seats along the road.
These "reservations" seem to be made with anything that
comes to hand, dirty newspapers, plastic bags, and old mats
with stones on top. It always looks ugly and has, of course,
nothing to do with Baba's teachings. People even rose at 2 A.M.
to reserve seats. One early morning, I got so annoyed at this
scene, that I—with the help of a couple of taxi drivers who had
parked their cars on the road—collected it all in a heap and
put a match to it. To no avail, the next day, it was the same!

One day that summer, Baba entered the hall for the first
morning darshan as if hesitating—he almost seemed to stagger
at the entrance. It looked, for a brief moment, as if he was
about to lose his balance when he leaned against the door
frame. I thought to myself that the vibrations meeting him
from all those sitting in the hall may not have been all that
pleasant.

But Baba was quickly in full command and walked to a lady sitting in the front saying, "Very bad, very bad." He looked very stern and she looked as if she wished the floor would open up and swallow her. Alternatively, a look from him can flash like lightening across the hall and hit the center of your being, transporting you to another dimension of consciousness. In that center is something alive, probably the soul, and it vibrates so sweetly at this contact.

All of a sudden a lemon flew from Baba's hand across the room. In his usual style, with a circular wave of the hand — it seemed to emerge from thin air, but in fact it was nothing less than an act of creation. It landed in the hands of a lady from a far off country. Baba, of course, was aware of the service work she had done, and this was a token of his acknowledgment. During a previous stay in Kodaikanal, I had seen Baba publicly reward a woman in a similar way. On that occasion two girls had checked into a five-star hotel in Bangalore, falsely saying the bill for their stay would be taken care of by Baba. When the time came to settle the account, there was nobody to pay it. The woman prevented a disgraceful situation by paying the bill herself. Baba was completely aware of the incident and acknowledged her action. Who can fathom his omniscience? Certainly not the human mind.

After morning darshan, Baba often went out in his car to be driven slowly along the road around the lake. He probably needed a breather from all the devotees who more or less besieged his house for hours, long after the gates had been closed indicating it was time to go home. Baba gave several hints that he could do without this behavior, but the crowds stayed on, even waiting for his car to return. And this after they had just had his darshan. I sometimes think they would devour him if they could. But it is not the outer contact with Baba's human form, however charming and gracious that may be, that matters so much as the inner contact with the divinity he is. It is this that leads to a nobler, more dignified and refined pattern of behavior.

A Kuja
of Water

Often Westerners visiting India make remarks about the appearance of ordinary village people, many of whom are from the poorest strata of society. They complain that these people are not too clean, and that prices seem to go up whenever they buy from them. But they forget that most Indian villages do not have the luxury of running water that pours from a tap, with little effort, and less thought, whenever it is required. On the contrary, people often have to walk long distances to get a *kuja* (an Indian pot) of water from a hand pump, which they then must carry home on their heads or hips. That meager, hard won water has to last as a day's supply for a big family of parents, children, and relatives.

As far as money is concerned, the exchange rate for foreign currency in India is embarrassingly high, with sterling and the US dollar eagerly sought. Under the circumstances, can these unfortunate people, who often are lucky to get one meal a day, and for millions of whom the sky is the only roof they have over their heads, be blamed for trying to take advantage of the situation? If Westerners were in the shoes of Indian villagers and peasants, would the Westerners behave any differently?

We Could All Pack Up If—

Each day throughout Baba's delightful stay in the beauty of the Indian mountains at Kodaikanal, there are bhajans in the evening. Swami sits on his chair on the dais and pours his divinity out over everyone. As you leave the hall after bhajans, you can see clearly on most faces that all inner knots have been loosened. The expressions are all of harmony and peace.

But outside the compound there is always the shock of the dirty newspapers and mats that people leave to "book" a place in line. They don't even bother to collect them afterward. The papers are left to pollute the lovely natural setting right next to the Divine's house.

Even the beautiful lake nearby has been polluted by plastic bags and other garbage thrown into it. It is a disgraceful sight despite signs erected by the local municipal authorities saying, "Ask not what the mountains can do for you, ask what you have done unto these mountains," and "Clean Kodai, Green Kodai."

But unless the Sai organization, or local authorities, do something prohibiting the placing of material on the public road to "book" places during Baba's stay, this shameful scene in front of Swami's house is not likely to change. It is quite distressing for those who take Baba's teachings seriously.

Typically, the last day of Baba's stay in Kodaikanal ends with bhajans in the evening that arise like a hymn of thanksgiving that "thou art." Without the divine in our midst at this critical time — which has been referred to as "the hour of God" — we might as well all pack up and silently creep away into the surrounding darkness.

The
Swiss Clock

On the last evening of my stay at Kodaikanal in 1991, a volunteer worker announced in a low, reserved voice, "There will be no darshan tomorrow morning. Swami is leaving for Ooty at 7:00 A.M." This was unusual because normally it is never announced when Baba is leaving, otherwise he would have a whole cortege of vehicles following his car. It is fairly well-known that following Baba's car, without permission or a special invitation to do so, is not allowed. Not everyone knows this of course, but once having been made aware of it, no devotee would think of doing so. Swami, though, sometimes has his own way of inviting devotees to follow him.

After the announcement I booked a taxi for 6:00 A.M. next morning, to be on the road to Ooty before Swami's own departure. That evening one of the volunteer workers had given me a small piece of a jasmine garland that had been used to decorate Baba's chair on the dais in the bhajan hall. I put it on my pillow as I went to bed and awoke, after a refreshing sleep, completely recovered from a cold that had been bothering me for several days. When I looked at my clock it was 5:00 A.M., and suddenly there was a knock on the door. A voice called, "It's 6:00 A.M., madam, your taxi is here." I replied quickly, "You are wrong, your watch is one hour too fast." But the boy outside insisted that his version of the time was correct. A check with my neighbor in the lodge showed he was right. It was 6:03 A.M. on my neighbor's clock and 5:03 A.M. on mine! I couldn't believe it. My reliable Swiss clock had never let me down before, and being an hour behind was very strange indeed. To add to my embarrassment I had arranged to pick up two other passengers on my way out of Kodaikanal.

As a result, I did not leave until 6:50 A.M., ten minutes before Baba's scheduled departure. I picked up my companions, and we stopped at the foot of the hill for a drink of coconut water. At that moment "Love" drove up. "Love" is the name devotees have given to Baba's red Mercedes Benz, just the right vehicle for the godhead he is. The car stopped for a few minutes, and as we watched, Baba got out to bless a group of people waiting there. I knew immediately that the mysterious failure of my Swiss clock was one of Baba's sweet leelas, and an invitation to travel in company with him. We quickly jumped into our taxi and followed his car for the rest of the long journey to Ooty.

To be in a vehicle following Baba's car is a special treat. Our taxi seemed filled with his energy. Every sight along the way was seen much more keenly. The trees along the road took on a beauty they had never had before. No one spoke. No one wanted to break the highly charged silence. Twice along the way Baba stopped at the homes of faithful devotees to pay short visits, while we waited outside under the shade of trees in the sticky heat of the plains.

At the second visit we lost track of Baba when he left. There were so many by-roads it was impossible to see which one he had taken. But one of the ever helpful *Seva Dals* (volunteer workers), with the familiar blue scarf around his neck, popped his head through the open window of our taxi and said, "Go straight, then turn right." We followed his directions and soon found "Love" again.

I have always found that you can completely rely on the Seva Dals. The famous scarf stands for a high level of integrity and gives these people a stature and authority that I have never seen misused. For gentlemen the scarves are in two blue colors radiating out from the Sathya Sai symbol in the center, and ladies have the same design but in orange.

About halfway to Ooty our driver had to pull into a service station to get some gas. In no time, of course, Baba's car was completely out of sight and everything abruptly appeared so flat. While we were waiting for the tank to be filled, I repeatedly sent a silent call to Baba, "Please wait for us, Swami. Wait." Several kilometers further along the road there he was, waiting.

Some people had gathered by the roadside where he stopped his car and I am sure he blessed them. But I felt distinctly that he had heard my call and was waiting for us to catch up. As soon as our taxi was back behind his car, he continued the journey.

One of the other passengers in the taxi, who had protested at the beginning of our journey behind Baba, certainly changed her mind along the way. "*Es war wahnsinnig gut*" (It was fantastic), she said the next day. She admitted that she had almost started crying when our taxi pulled in for gas and lost sight of Baba's car, because she thought our treat was over.

It was a delightful trip and none of us felt any of the strain and fatigue that usually accompanies a seven-and-a-half hour car drive. On the contrary, feeling fresh and relaxed on arriving at Ooty, I took a motorized rickshaw up to Baba's school to attend a late afternoon darshan and enjoy sitting in the serene peace of that lovely place.

Baba's Shiva Aspect

It is a great privilege for a devotee to be living at the feet of the divine, but it also entails great responsibility. You must be careful to control and discipline your behavior. I have seen Baba demonstrate this clearly when, for example, he spoke very sternly to some ladies, sitting right in front of him, before the start of bhajans one night at Ooty. In a most severe tone, he pointed out their disregard for the guidelines that have been laid down to maintain order and a harmonious atmosphere, such as "Do not reserve space for yourself or others on any occasion," and "Keep your surroundings clean and orderly."

"You have no character," Baba said. He spoke with great intensity, and coming from him that is about the strongest condemnation possible. His whole teaching is founded on character building. All ancient Indian scriptures hold a person's character above all. "*Sadhana* (spiritual discipline) without the base of character is like the journey of a blind man," Baba says.

Apparently referring to the behavior of devotees a few days earlier at Kodaikanal, when they polluted the lovely natural setting outside his residence, Baba said, "Where is the bhakti (*devotion*) in this?" Each word was like the blow from a hammer. No doubt he was also referring in broader terms to devotees' lack of care for the environment and general lack of consideration for others.

He said many other things that night at Ooty that demonstrated he knew about every detail of devotees' conduct. For example he asked one lady in a severe voice, "Where is your visa?" To another he simply said, "Go," and asked the Seva Dals to show the person out of the hall. To use his own expression, his approach to the whole issue was as "hard as a diamond."

It was wonderful and awe inspiring to see Baba's Shiva aspect so strongly. Shiva is the third God of the Hindu trinity, the others being Brahma the creator and Vishnu the preserver. Shiva is said to have a destructive capacity that is used to clear away the old to make way for the new. He is the one who points us to the correct path; it is up to us to choose it or not. Baba's teachings stand for nobility and a loving heart that mean purity in thought, word, and deed. But in fact, it is often possible to see the opposite even among those who claim to be long-time devotees.

If, instead of human pettiness, devotees had in their minds a little of the grandeur and expansion of the mountains in Ooty, where Baba expressed his disapproval of their behavior, particularly in Kodaikanal, they would seem to be on the right path. During bhajans that evening in Ooty I saw Baba wipe a tear from his cheek.

I have now been with Swami for eight years, but this is the only time I have seen him be so severe. This reveals the wonderful true and uncompromising aspect of his divinity. Divine love is not sentimentality but pure and unconditional.

Baba says: "The mind is like a boulder which the intellect transforms into an image even as a sculptor does. If the intellect allows the senses to dictate the design, the stone will be shaped into a horrid idol; if, however, the senses are sublimated by the spirit, the image wrought by the intellect will be simply adorable. One must have the mind fully co-operating in the spiritual discipline and not obstructing the process at every step. Liberation is the goal, and the mind must help the pilgrim at every stage of this journey. Mind should not admit any activity that is contrary to dharma or injurious to spiritual progress."

Swami's teachings are heralding the breakthrough of a new world order where all the brutality and tyranny of this world is being transformed, and his exquisite message is beginning to be actualized.

What is Divine Love?

During another stay at one of the mountain resorts Baba visits from time to time, someone in an interview asked, "What is divine love?" Baba gave a beautiful description of "this eternal power" as being an expression of divine consciousness and at the very core of creation itself.

During his explanation, however, Baba did not mention that the manifestation of divine love in this world, which is full of ignorance and darkness, is the greatest sacrifice, the highest form of self-giving. How could it be otherwise? One look at Baba's own life of uninterrupted self-giving is proof enough.

This power of his divine love is so pure and so mighty that coming in contact with it uplifts our whole being. Compared with its light, so-called human love, always pre-occupied with itself, seems a rather bizarre imitation. There is really only one thing to do. We must expand human love—which is perhaps more like desire since we love our possessions and status—into genuine selfless love. Without this kind of love, there can be no pure spiritual life.

Divine love is Swami's weapon against the forces of evil. Evil is unable to touch him. Though sometimes, in order to save a devotee's life, Swami will take upon himself an evil force such as a fatal disease. In such cases it appears to become absorbed into his being and has been known to give him a high fever.

Divine love is Swami's instrument to bring about much needed change in human nature, as he emphasizes in practically all his discourses. It is the basic thing he asks of us, that we change, and it can be very difficult. For example, it can be tough for a chain smoker, or someone who eats too much, to break the habit of a lifetime. "Loading, loading," Swami said to one devotee who suffered from the weakness of overeating.

It is the habits of attachments that have to be broken if we are to clear a pathway for the divine's power to enter us and do its work. Naturally this transformation becomes much easier through a personal contact with the godhead himself. Such a relationship can even make the path sunlit, although at times there are sure to be clouds, for Swami is a strict taskmaster.

The godhead himself is not, however, too happy about our progress. "Time has come for you to act," he said to a devotee who was a private guest at his mountain residence. "You use a lot of words, but you do not act." On another occasion, at Prasanthi Nilayam, Baba said he was not satisfied with the level of service work being performed. What are we waiting for? We know the path. The signposts that indicate the correct direction have been erected. We know the goal. We have come from the Divine and we must return to the Divine.

Easwaramma Day

I was privileged to be at Kodaikanal one year when Easwaramma Day was celebrated there. Easwaramma is the name of Baba's mother, who was born in 1890 and died on May 6, 1972. Both Baba's parents are honored by a shrine a short distance from the Prasanthi Nilayam Ashram. His mother had always shown special interest and fondness for children, writes Professor N. Kasturi in his book *Easwaramma — The Chosen Mother*,[1] so May 6 is celebrated as the Children's Day to honor Baba's mother.

It is well-known among longtime devotees that Swami can make the sun shine or the rain stop if he wants, and he had apparently ordered fine weather for this occasion. A class of Bal Vikas girls in white dresses, with white jasmine in their hair, sat at Baba's feet under a large photograph of Easwaramma that had been beautifully decorated with lilies and other flowers. Several talks were given, including a discourse by Baba in his native Telugu language, a great part of which was chanted. Even a mother's sweetest singing to her children could not have penetrated the innermost recesses of the heart as did Swami's voice that day, vibrating with such intense love.

Bal Vikas children are very special. Meeting them again reminded me of an international rally of Bal Vikas' children a

[1]N. Kasturi, *Easwaramma — The Chosen Mother* (Nilayam, 515134 Anatapur A. P., India: Sir Sathya Sai Publications, 1984).

few years earlier when about five thousand of them assembled at Prasanthi Nilayam. Each time Baba appeared, their joy knew no bounds. Their eyes shone in competition with the sun. In a parade at the big new Hill View Stadium, they all wore white dresses with navy blue belts and matching bonnets with yellow feathers in them. It was a picturesque sight, but above all, they all looked so happy.

Later when the children departed from the big tents and their campsite, toward the rear of the ashram, the whole area had been perfectly cleaned. There was not so much as a single banana peel left. They indeed lived up to Baba's saying, "Cleanliness is Godliness." The attitude of many adults toward cleaning up after themselves is such that I thought it unlikely the children had learned this conduct from their elders. It was more likely the other way around, that these small children were teaching their elders proper conduct.

In my experience the difference between the thousands of Bal Vikas children and children who have had a so-called modern education, is vast. To be in the presence of Bal Vikas children is a pleasure. Their behavior is calm and balanced, which can scarcely be said about many children educated under "modern" principles. In contrast, many modern children have bad attitudes and their conduct is undisciplined. These unhappy children may later in life—in their search for love and peace—take to drugs, alcohol, nicotine, a wide range of stimulants, or depressants, or the more publicized "hard" drugs, as a means of escape from a world they feel is barren.

In the Bal Vikas educational world the word "modern" has been replaced by the word "love." These children are brought up, first of all, to know and live the unselfish love of Baba.

Easwaramma Day is not only celebrated in honor of Baba's mother, perhaps more importantly it is a symbol to make the world aware of the fact that motherhood is something sacred. Baba has said that a mother, if she is aware of her responsibilities, is not only the backbone of the family but the backbone of the nation. He says that when the mother has been given her rightful place, there will be greater harmony in the world.

Though Baba was speaking in a small bhajan hall in the beauty of the Indian mountains, he was actually writing a new page in the history of humankind. He was accentuating and perpetuating an important aspect of his mission with the yearly celebration of Easwaramma Day—the sacredness of motherhood.

After Baba had concluded his Easwaramma talk, he spoke at length about people's lack of care for their surroundings. I felt that he was referring, at least in part, to the situation outside his house in Kodaikanal, which each year is the same and with which he, by now, was annoyed. He said, "You don't care because there is no beauty in your hearts." I assumed these powerful words were his way of indicating not only that something should be done about the mess outside, but contained a firm message about the broader national and global issues of pollution and the widespread despoilation we have inflicted on the planet. Local people in the hall warmly approved of his statement by doing *namaskar* (holding the palms together) above their heads as he spoke.

After celebrating Easwaramma Day, Baba left for Ooty. On the way up the mountains to Ooty, through one sharp hairpin bend in the road after another, there is written on the many protruding rocks, "There is only one God, Jesus." There is only one god, but he has many names.

A Hindu Wedding

I was fortunate to be at Ooty the year Baba decided to inaugurate, on the last evening of his stay, a new hall built down the hill from the school. He had also agreed to marry a young Hindu couple in the hall the following day.

That night there was heavy traffic between the school and the hall as Seva Dal volunteers carried chandeliers, vases of flowers, and garlands of mango leaves to decorate the building. Mango leaves, when hung over the doorways, are considered to be very auspicious. The hall was of the same design, size, and shape as the so-called "sheds" at Prasanthi Nilayam that are used to accommodate devotees visiting the ashram.

For once, instead of the usual mad rush to get in, devotees entered decently, one by one, thanks mainly to Seva Dals in their blue scarves directing the stream of people wanting to attend the inauguration. The ceremony was simple but moving, and sitting in the hall, I had a strange feeling that something extraordinary was taking place. Baba, sitting on his chair on the dais, was not so much inaugurating a new hall as a new era. It seemed that there really was a breakthrough now of the highest divine forces. The whole atmosphere of the place was electrifying.

Later, there was hectic activity at the school, and trucks began arriving with enormous *bartans* (pots and vessels) in which food was to be prepared for the wedding guests the next day. In the morning beating drums, pounded Indian style with incredible speed and rhythm, announced that two young people were to be married in the beautifully decorated hall with Baba conducting the ceremony.

By the time the groom arrived, the hall was packed with people. He was dressed in a beige silk dhoti and silk vest, and accompanied by family and close friends. The bride followed, also with family and friends. She wore a bonnet of jasmine flowers that completely covered her hair and trailed in a long plait down her back, a brocade sari, jewelry, and a diadem on her forehead. She looked very pretty. The bride and groom took their places under an illuminated canopy over the dais and everyone waited for Baba to arrive and perform the ceremony.

As Swami approached the hall, under a silk turquoise umbrella held aloft to protect him from the sun, Seva Dals formed lines to control the crowds. People rushed to follow his progress, some even tumbling head over heels down the hill, to be in his presence when he entered the hall. He walked up the aisle, taking letters from devotees, and that supreme hand of his that has performed so many wonders was held up to bless the guests—numbering somewhere between six and eight hundred.

Baba sat smiling in his chair on the left of the dais as priests chanted mantras and traditional Hindu rituals were performed. Then he rose and, with that familiar circling motion of his hand, created a beautiful "thali" with a medallion (an auspicious necklace) to be worn by the bride. As it dropped from his palm he caught it with a quick movement of the hand. For a brief moment it hung from one of his fingers for all to see before he gave it to the groom, who placed the sacred necklace around the neck of the girl who was to be his wife.

Baba blessed them both—that they may have a happy life, and certainly if they pursue a spiritual life it will be full of bliss, regardless of outer circumstances. Swami only stayed in the hall about twenty minutes, but his presence had filled the entire hall and made the wedding a very beautiful experience. Afterward lunch was served for private guests under a *pandal* (booth) especially erected outside for the occasion.

Being in the mountains, it was a simple wedding, and its very simplicity was its great charm. A wedding down on the plains, at Whitefield for example, is a far more elaborate affair. There the hosts would arrange for the venue to be profusely decorated with flowers. Bells made of flowers would hang from the ceiling and garlands of flowers would stretch from wall to wall. The dais, where the couple to be married would sit, is also sumptuously adorned with flowers. The pathway from the mandir to the hall, along which Baba would walk, is often made of flowers rather than a red carpet. A marriage without flowers is a rather incomplete affair in India, and together with the beautiful silk or brocade saris worn by the ladies, makes a Hindu wedding an especially colorful ceremony.

Immediately after the wedding in Ooty, Baba departed for Whitefield. His sojourn on earth is the supreme sacrifice. There is not a single pause in it. After a snack, I left with some friends for the scenic drive back to Whitefield via Mysore, including several hours through the jungle near Mysore. The city is famous for the stunning palace built for the former Maharajah by the British. It is still occupied by his son. After lunch at the Ritz Hotel in Mysore—not quite as elegant as the hotel bearing the same name in Paris—we arrived back in Whitefield that evening.

The Dance
of the Gopis
in Modern Times

The new bhajan hall built at Kodaikanal in 1988 had already become too small by the summer of 1989 and needed an extension. And for devotees who followed Baba to the mountain resort for a few weeks' holiday, this unlikely setting was to become a symbolic re-enactment of the dance of the Gopis performed for Lord Krishna 5,000 years earlier.

Krishna of that time was a godhead just as is the Parthi Krishna of our time. In fact, Baba has revealed himself in the form of Krishna to at least one longtime devotee. Gopis were cowherds who worshipped Lord Krishna in Brindavan. They represent both the male and female aspect of the devotees of Lord Krishna.

But it was not milk and curd the modern gopis carried in their baskets for their Parthi Krishna, it was something far more substantial—soil and pieces of solid rock. Hired labor could have been used to extend the bhajan hall but the Lord chose to have the job done by his devotees. And what an opportunity it was for them. Many eager hands offered to help and joyfully the gopis swung the baskets from one pair of hands to another, forming either a circle or a long line, while Parthi Krishna symbolically played his flute of love to them. The godhead of Parthi may not have a real flute but his mere presence was music enough and had the same magic charm as the murali of Krishna must have had 5,000 years ago.

Silhouetted against the clear blue sky, Swami looked on as he walked back and forth on the large balcony of his Kodaikanal home, a picturesque figure in an orange robe contrasting with his big crown of black hair. He stood, with a few tall eucalyptus trees in the background, clapping his hands in his usual captivating manner to keep time with the singing and "dancing" of the gopis below. As their voices soared upward in a chorus of "Krishna, Krishna Jai," he filled them all with his joy and energy.

In this extraordinarily beautiful scene on a steep hillside in Kodaikanal, with the sun reflecting off the waters of the lake and surrounded by lush, tropical vegetation, the devotees worked away happily. Tirelessly, these modern day gopis moved piles of earth from one point to another, some sending their baskets flying to bridge a deep cleft in the clay and mud wall, others skillfully passing their baskets to the next in line.

What a contrast to how these things are usually done in India! Normally women workers would be used, walking erect with the easy grace of a ballet dancer so as not to spill any of the load they carry in baskets on their heads. After a long day of hard toil, they would be paid a pittance by western standards.

The daily routine for devotees was about two hours *seva* (selfless service) in the morning, after which all were served with a delicious treat of Indian sweets and pasteurized, cardamom flavored milk in cartons. In the afternoons there was another two hours seva before evening bhajans. This routine continued for about eight-to-ten days.

Even on Easwaramma Day this "dance" continued under the flags and festoons that had been erected for the occasion. In the morning on the festival day there was a short bhajan session in honor of the woman who gave birth to a divine child. In the afternoon, the seva continued for her son, now a world renowned godhead.

That evening, the compound was packed with devotees who had been arriving in a steady stream since early morning. They joyfully sang "Krishna Jai Krishna Jai" and other bhajans. When the holy songs ended, Krishna Parthi, the embodiment of all that is good and divine in this life and the hereafter, blessed everyone and retired to his house.

Two of the charming gopis, friends and traveling companions of mine from Italy and Greece who now live with their families in South Africa, received a special farewell gift from *Gopala* (another name for Lord Krishna) on the day of their departure. With a beaming smile, he approached where they were sitting during bhajans, made a sign to them to get up, and gave each of them a stack of vibhuti packets. One of them took with both her hands not the gift, but the hand that gave it. She bent over and kissed Swami's hand, expressing with this spontaneous gesture the gratitude that many of the gopis felt in their hearts. The job they had done had been good for both body and mind.

By May 7, walls had been neatly cut and the space cleared for the extension to the bhajan hall. Next day, Swami left for Ooty. Ooty and Kodaikanal are the two places in the mountains that Swami visits each year during the hot season. In Ooty, Baba materialized a lingam on the birthday of the great Indian philosopher, Shankara. A lingam is the symbol of Shiva, as well as of creation and protection, and therefore it could be said, represents Baba himself. It had the size and shape of an egg. Swami held it aloft, between his forefinger and thumb, for everyone to see. The lingam was transparent, with light playing inside it in various colors.

In the towns all the way to Ooty, in the Nilgiri Hills, immense crowds lined the road to greet the avatar as he passed by. It occurred to me that it was beginning to dawn on the people of India that Sri Venkateswara (another name for Vishnu, the divine protector) was in their midst leading their country toward a great destiny.

The day after I returned from Ooty, I was sitting cross-legged under the circular roof of the bhajan mandap at Whitefield writing down my recent experiences, when suddenly I felt two soft lips pressing against my cheek. It was a kiss from a small Indian boy, 3 or 4 years old. As I was about to question the boy about his boldness, the thought struck me that Swami was just a short distance away, inside the mandir, and it might be his leela and a token of his love. A smile quickly replaced my surprised expression.

"They Invest
in the Soul"

While reading a Scandinavian newspaper, I came across a full-page article with the intriguing headline, "They Invest in the Soul." The article stated that psychoanalysis was no longer the sole prerogative of the East Coast of the USA and middle-class America, that Scandinavia was about to get its own class of "soul doctors." Apparently, it costs a fortune to go to these psychoanalysts. The article claimed people often had to take out a bank loan to afford the costly treatment, and if the therapist and the patient were not matched psychologically, the treatment was doomed to failure even after a hundred sessions.

It occurred to me that perhaps the treatment was doomed to failure under any circumstances. Surely it is a lot healthier for the soul to "invest" in its own freedom by learning to live from within, to act from within, and to establish contact with the inner being that is the real truth of our existence. One sure way to regain the health of mind and body is to curtail desires. Our relentless pursuit of more and more material wealth—in the mistaken belief that if we had just one more thing we could be happy—is one of the greatest enemies of mental well-being and the development of the soul.

To delve into the depths of the subconscious, without bringing down the light from a higher consciousness may do more harm than good, according to Sri Aurobindo. We must ask ourselves who is there, among all those who claim to be therapists, who actually has contact with higher conscious-ness and therefore, can bring down the light. This is extremely difficult to do. University degrees in medicine or psychology are not necessarily much help. What is needed is a high degree of inner purity—then the contact with the higher consciousness can be established. This is and has been done by some therapists around the world. Baba shows how it can be done.

Sri Aurobindo also shed light on the subject when he wrote: "Our highly activistic and one-sided culture is faced with a crisis that may end in self-destruction because it lacks the inner depth of an authentic spiritual consciousness. With-out such depth our moral and political protestations are just verbiage. Without an authentic spiritual consciousness, today's psychoanalysis may end in the ditch."[2]

To one disciple Sri Aurobindo said, "Your practice of psycho-analysis was a mistake. It has, for the time at least, made the work of purification more complicated, not easier. . . . It takes up a certain part, the darkest, the most perilous, the unhealthiest part of the nature, the lower vital subcon-scious layer, . . . and attributes to it . . . an action out of all proportion to its true role in the nature. . . . As in all infant sciences, the universal habit of the human mind—to take a partial or local truth, generalise it unduly and try to explain a whole field of Nature in its narrow terms—runs riot here."[3]

Sri Aurobindo continues, "I find it difficult to take these psycho-analysts at all seriously when they try to scrutinize spiritual experience by the flicker of their torch-lights,—yet perhaps one ought to, for half-knowledge is a powerful thing and can be a great obstacle to the coming in front of the Truth. This new psychology looks to me very much like chil-

[2]Sri Aurobindo, *Letters on Yoga*, Vol. 2 (Pondicherry, India: Sri Aurobindo Ashram Trust, 1970), p. 1605.
[3]Sri Aurobindo, *Letters on Yoga*, Vol. 3 (Pondicherry, India: Sri Aurobindo Ashram Trust, 1979), p. 1605, 1906.

dren learning some summary and not very adequate alpha-
bet, exulting in putting their a-b-c-d of the subconscient and
the mysterious underground super-ego together and imagin-
ing that their first book of obscure beginnings . . . is the very
heart of real knowledge. They look from down up and
explain the higher lights by the lower obscurities; but the
foundation of these things is above and not below. . . . The
significance of the lotus is not to be found by analysing the
secrets of the mud from which it grows here; its secret is to be
found in the heavenly archetype of the lotus that blooms for
ever in the Light above. The self-chosen field of these psy-
chologists is besides poor, dark and limited."[4]

"None is more ignorant, more perilous, more unreason-
ing and obstinate in recurrence than the lower vital subconscious and its movements. To raise it up prematurely or
improperly for *anubhara* is to risk suffusing the conscious
parts also with its dark and dirty stuff and thus poisoning the
whole vital and even the mental nature. Always therefore one
should begin by a positive not a negative experience, by
bringing down something of the divine nature, calm, light,
equanimity, purity, divine strength into the parts of the conscious being that have to be changed; only when that has
been sufficiently done and there is a firm positive basis, is it
safe to raise up the concealed subconscious adverse elements
in order to destroy and eliminate them. . . . Then they can be
dealt with with much less danger and under a higher internal
guidance.[5]

"You must know the whole before you can know the
part and the highest before you can truly understand the
lowest. That is the promise of the greater psychology awaiting its hour before which these poor gropings will disappear
and come to nothing."[6]

---

[4]Sri Aurobindo, *Letters on Yoga*, Vol. 3, pp. 1608, 1609.
[5]Sri Aurobindo, *Letters on Yoga*, Vol. 3, p. 1608.
[6]Sri Aurobindo, *Letters on Yoga*, Vol. 3, p. 1609.

Baba, too, has expressed a view about psychoanalysis. In a recent interview he asked, "Are there any psychoanalysts here?" Satisfied that there were not, he went on to say in his simple yet powerful style, "They use tricks. Do not go to them."

The way we live in the world today provokes such great turmoil and disharmony that human beings become exhausted both physically and mentally. We develop ulcers from tension and faulty hearts from strain. We eat too much, sleep too little, and work too hard. That leads to nervous disorders and breakdowns. We then turn to psychoanalysis and all manner of psychological techniques to try and find the security we have lost because God has been forgotten. Psychoanalysis, as it is widely practiced, may well be the last thing we should associate with spiritual life. The most direct way to heal mind and body is to listen and most of all, live the words of Baba, the godman of our time.

The divine does take care of a devotee's welfare. He has proved it thousands of times to devotees all over the world. But this doesn't mean you can sit back in a rocking chair, comfortably rocking back and forth, thinking that everything will be done for you. On the contrary, your responsibility is to live his message of harmony in a world that is totally out of balance, and the closer you draw to the divine, the greater that responsibility becomes.

Baba's countless leelas have a double purpose. First, they prove his divinity, for his leelas are on such a grand scale, often saving many a devotee's life, that only the divine could have performed them. The second reason for their manifestation is to influence us to change and become human, for as Baba says, "Without living the human values, you are not men but devils."

Baba's message of unity among human beings, communities, nations, and East and West is spreading fast and there is now compelling evidence, unimaginable even a few short years ago, that the world is moving toward a better future of harmony and co-operation.

Baba's Sankalpa

An Indian gentleman who works as a librarian in one of Swami's colleges became very indignant when his bicycle was stolen. "After all," he said, "I have come here only for Swami's sake and to work for him." He seemed to think it was Swami's duty to see that such a thing should not happen. But he had left the bicycle unlocked outside his house and should have known better. In India you cannot do that without running the risk that the bicycle will disappear. To my mind, it had little or nothing to do with Swami's *sankalpa* (divine will) and was simply the result of carelessness.

In the same way if anyone visiting the ashram at Puttaparthi gets a fever, it is immediately assumed that it is Swami who is "cleaning them out." If someone is infected with jaundice, again Baba is blamed—rather than the devotee accepting responsibility for the illness. It is true that Swami does "clean out" people who come to him, but it is certainly not the rule. In these cases people go through a kind of purification process, which can be very unpleasant, and on rare occasions they develop a fever.

But the fact is many devotees leave the ashram to go outside for a cup of coffee or to sample the local cuisine in the village of Puttaparthi, where standards of hygiene are very different from the West. As in most Indian villages, there is no running water. Cups and eating utensils are washed throughout the day in the same bucket of water that is soon swimming with all kinds of germs. Two very common diseases in India are TB and jaundice, and there is always a danger of picking up intestinal worms and amoebas resulting in severe diarrhea. I find it very difficult to see how all this can have anything to do with Baba "cleaning people out," as is commonly thought. It is more likely a natural consequence of disregarding elementary sanitary rules when traveling in a country like India, where clear water is hard to obtain, and hygienic standards are consequently difficult to raise.

What are we to think when the divine allows himself to suffer the natural consequences of an accident, as he did in August, 1988? On a Saturday morning, Baba slipped on a piece of soap in his bathroom, fell on his back, and sustained a fracture to the hip bone. The injury he suffered was a natural consequence of the fall, as natural as heat is generated by fire. Whoever sustains a fall, whether it is Swami or anybody else, will suffer from the consequent injury. Even the divine, when he is in human form, submits himself to the laws governing nature.

Here is what Baba said, shortly after the incident, during a talk in the Poornanchandra auditorium: "The body is subject to ailments from time to time. It comes and goes. If I rid myself of any ailment instantaneously people may comment, What a selfish person is Sai Baba. He cures his illness immediately. But he does not remove the pain of others.

"Whether it is your bodily ailment or somebody else's, attempts can be made to treat it, to teach the sufferer how to control the mind, and strengthen the powers of resistance. But it cannot be got rid of the same instant. The time required has to be allowed. It is to teach this lesson to you that I chose to speak to you today. At all times and in all situations recite the name of the Lord with devotion. Live in harmony and love with everyone. The Lord's name is sweeter than nectar. Let the Lord's sweet name dance on your tongue."

It is not as easy as it may sound, but it is a great help in *Sadhana* (spiritual practice). That day Baba concluded his talk by singing a bhajan. When his voice rings out it calls to us to live a better and nobler life, it almost seems to lift the roof of the vast Poornachandra Auditorium—so mighty and powerful are its vibrations.

The Doctor
of Prasanthi Nilayam

While visiting Prasanthi Nilayam, a friend came down with amoebic dysentery, a dreadful infection that is almost impossible to cure. No medication she took was of any help. She became thinner and thinner until she was virtually skin and bones and looked twenty years older. One day as she was resting on the balcony in front of her room, beginning to think she didn't have much longer to live, a gentleman whom she did not know and had never seen before approached her.

"You are sick," he said. "How do you know?" she replied, somewhat reserved, "Are you a doctor at the hospital?" "No," he replied, "I am the doctor of Prasanthi Nilayam. Here, take these two pills, one in the evening and one in the morning and you will be all right."

My friend took the pills as prescribed and recovered relatively quickly, then gradually regained her normal weight. The whole incident was witnessed by her roommate, who was sitting inside at the time and who was equally perplexed as to the identity of the mysterious "doctor." It is worth noting that there is in fact, no official ashram doctor. There are doctors at Sai Baba's hospital next door to the ashram grounds, but none of them would think of describing themselves as "the doctor of Prasanthi Nilayam."

A Fifty Rupee Note

Baba's leelas are all an expression of his power or energy and therefore are unlimited. He himself is the unlimited. Devotees who have experienced his omniscience and omnipresence are left speechless. Yet the greatest of all his wonders is himself. Each time you are brought either directly or indirectly into contact with his sublime reality, your heart is filled with intense gratitude that the divine does exist, that the world is not just the apparent trouble and turmoil it seems—that there is the divine.

Here is a small example of his leelas that I experienced. The remittance of a sum of money from abroad was delayed an unusually long time and finally I literally didn't have any money at all on which to live. I was reluctant to ask anyone for a loan, but I did want to send a cable to the bank asking that the delay be investigated. My problem was, where was I to get the money required to pay for sending the cable? With these thoughts running through my mind, I took a walk along the path beside the northern wall of the Whitefield ashram. Suddenly I became aware of something glimmering in the sand. I almost stepped on it, but there was no mistake. It was a fifty rupee note. Except for a couple of beggars, there was no one in sight. Realizing it was Swami's leela, I picked it up and went straight to the post office to send that cable.

That evening there were no bhajans, as Swami had gone out, so I decided to sit quietly by myself for a while in the ashram compound. At that point, an Indian lady I had never seen before came along and sat down beside me. She seemed keen to talk and told me she was from Madras and married to the captain of a cargo ship. She discussed her family's life under Baba's guidance and said, "He can be very strict, but he has made our life meaningful."

At first I took our chance meeting to be a coincidence, but I was soon to learn otherwise. She was a charming person so I shared with her my experience that morning. On hearing of my difficulties she smiled, took out her purse, and handed me a bundle of notes. "Here, one thousand rupees, you had better take it," she said. The next morning the lady left for home after giving me the number of her bank account in Madras. Needless to say, I quickly transferred the money back to her as soon as my remittance arrived.

Who, anywhere in the world, let alone India, would give such a sum of money to a person they had never met or even seen before? I had not even asked Swami for help, but he knew. It takes a little time to get used to the leelas of the omniscient divinity! However this incident is typical of the way he arranges things and to try and explain his leelas, or even doubt them, is absurd.

Evening Talks
at Whitefield

Evening talks at Whitefield are a relatively new part of the activities that take place around Baba, and they are very special. They take place inside the compound, in the big kaliana mandap hall, which can seat about a thousand people. Devotees wait in lines to enter the hall, with the first in each line drawing a number from a small bag to decide the order of entry. When people have seated themselves, cross-legged on the floor, the students and their teachers enter toward the front of the hall, and at the very front are those who work for Baba or in some way contribute to the spread of his message. Males sit to the right of the hall and females to the left, leaving an aisle down the center. The hall is usually packed, but no one talks. Everyone is waiting for Baba. Suddenly a whisper will run through the hall, "Swami is coming," or simply, "Swami." It is a magnetic word. Everybody instinctively makes last minute adjustments to his or her appearance and sitting position. Baba appreciates people making an effort to be at their best. All seem to draw a little closer to the front. Sometimes children leave their mothers and go forward, as though they cannot get close enough to Baba.

The moment Baba appears in the doorway all hands are raised, palms together, in *namaskar* to greet him. He manages to look innocent, almost surprised, as if he is totally unaware of the suspense he has kept everyone in as they have waited for perhaps half an hour. He will sometimes exchange a few words with someone sitting at the entrance, or take a walk down the long aisle in the middle of the hall. No doubt those sitting closest to him long to do *padnamaskar* (touching of the feet) but no one dares as he has clearly indicated he doesn't wish it. Intuitively you bow inwardly to this great divinity as he passes by. He sometimes takes a letter here and there, or listens to someone who speaks a few earnest words to him, then returns to his chair at the end of the hall.

Usually he sits quietly for a few minutes, as if gathering everyone in the hall into his protecting presence. It is difficult to describe the soothing peace that emanates from that presence. It envelopes the entire hall, penetrates everyone's heart. He sits in his chair with an outer appearance of massive calm, but underneath there burns a mighty fire. Perhaps he may take a letter from a student sitting at his feet and read it attentively, nodding a few times while doing so as if he approves of the contents.

Sometimes people will ask for vibhuti. Occasionally, after he has materialized it with a few circling movements of his hand, he will take a letter from the stack lying unread on the small table next to his chair and tear a piece off to fashion a packet to hold the vibhuti. Some are shocked at this. How can he do it when he has not even read the letter! But Baba has shown many times he knows the contents of a letter without reading it. Sometimes he will reply to what has been written without even having taken the letter at all. I have personally experienced this twice. He gave precise answers to my questions in letters that he did not take, and even repeated his replies to ensure they were not misunderstood. His answers were clearly heard by devotees sitting around me.

If Baba were to physically read the hundreds of letters that are given to him daily, he would have to spend the entire day just reading letters. The mere fact that he takes a letter is, for most devotees, a token of his blessings of its contents.

Many letters that are offered are not taken, and some are taken then quickly thrown back for some reason known only to Swami.

Eventually the student chosen to give the opening talk comes forward, but first he approaches Baba to perform *pad-namaskar* and generally receives an encouraging pat on the back. Most students step up to the microphone and address the audience of mostly adults whom they have never seen before, without a trace of stage fright. They talk in a natural and straightforward way, as though speaking to a friend, and with an eloquence that many a trained speaker would envy. Usually two or three other students also give either improvised or prepared talks. None of them ever use a prepared text or notes. Occasionally a student will become nervous in front of the big audience and struggle for words. But he is sure to get an encouraging nod from Baba, or a sign to leave the microphone and kneel at Baba's feet for an extra pat on the back. Most of the students are very bright, and many display fine leadership qualities. Their talks are always lively and engrossing.

On one such evening I recall hearing a boy describe the struggle he had been going through to, as he said, "undo the former pattern of sophistication and arrogance, to become whole and straight." Another student told of sitting in the hall doing examinations with no supervisor in attendance. No student would think of copying from another, "as we all feel the divine's eye is resting upon us," and he would surely know if anyone was copying. No doubt Swami is not so much their external as their internal examiner.

One student spoke of an experience Baba had during his schools days, which Swami subsequently described to the students himself. Baba sat on a bench between two friends, Ramesh and Prakash, who both loved him dearly. Wherever Baba went, they too were there. When Baba left the school, the two boys could not bear life without him — one drowned himself in a well and the other went mad.

Several years later, when Baba moved into the newly built temple at Prasanthi Nilayam, he acquired two dogs called Jack and Jill. At night one slept at the head of Baba's bed, while the other slept at the foot of the bed. Baba explained that the souls of those two village boys inhabited the forms of Jack and Jill. It was, apparently, the only way they could be in his immediate presence.

One day Swami sent Jack out to look after something, but the dog took shelter from the merciless Indian sun by settling under a car. Unfortunately when the car drove away, the dog was run over. Jack was badly mutilated but managed to drag himself back to Swami where he expired at his master's feet. Listening to these young people speak, I had the vivid impression that there are many Jack and Jills among Baba's students—beautiful souls who are completely devoted to their master. And Swami is the most indulgent master imaginable, full of love.

"There is never a need for a shadow of fear to enter our relationship with him. We need never be afraid of him. To borrow Shakespeare's phrase, he teaches us 'to be or not to be.' Life with Swami is not an ordinary life; it is a life full of challenges. Life in the everyday world can dull our sensitivity and turn us to 'stone,' but Swami uses his chisel of love to chip away the granite-like exterior and reveal the beautiful, integrated personality within," said a student one evening.

One boy raised his hand and asked permission to speak. Swami invited him to the microphone. In amazing command of the situation and himself, he told of a stay he and other students had enjoyed with Baba in the mountains at Kodaikanal. He said, "We were given intensive guidance in the spiritual life. Swami talked with us several times daily. And how he pampered us. One of us was ill in bed. Swami went personally to his room with a cup of coffee and also materialized some medicine for him. Staff members of the ashram and some top executives from companies in the West were Swami's private guests. He looked after them like a brother and perfect host."

The young man continued, "Today's youth has gone amok. Grownups have gone amok. For us to be here is the greatest opportunity there can be. Here we learn the way to live. Our aim in whatever we study is excellence. Our tuition is free. Food—everything—is free. There are no laboratory fees." (Most universities charge students a fee for the use of their scientific laboratories.) He concluded his talk with the words, "Bhagavan you are the master of my fate, you are the captain of my soul." He then bowed down before his captain who gave him a loving pat on the back.

Like a golden thread running through all the talks by male and female students, and some adults, is their love and adoration for Baba. And the students do their master great credit. For example, when the lady Vice-Chancellor of Mysore University gave a very inspired talk one evening, a boy was able to get up spontaneously and, in the most eloquent and warm terms, thank her for what she had said.

Few can doubt Baba's divine powers, which have conferred joy on thousands of people all over the world. Yet the greatest miracle he performs is the transformation he brings about in people. I have seen hundreds of young students transformed, and it is this change he is bringing about in youth, in particular, that augers well for the future of the world. The transformation he works in us makes us better students and more dutiful citizens. He is imbuing the student community with a high sense of duty, devotion, and discipline. His boundless grace and mercy turn vagrant youth into sincere seekers. Swami's educational institutions have become a haven of refuge for the young against the terrible onslaughts of materialism.

"I believe we cannot even conceive the magnitude of debt we owe Swami. He has not only changed the life style of students, he has conferred on us all a fresh new life. His love and mercy have turned those who were not even worth the dust from which they were made into people who are worth their weight in gold," were the reflections of another student.

Often on Sundays at Whitefield, the master himself gives a talk—his words accompanied by lively and expressive movements of those beautifully sculptured hands. In a more private talk to students in recent years, Baba told them that the father of his next incarnation, as Prema Sai, had been born in the southern Indian state of Karnataka. He also said that the body of Prema Sai was in the process of being formed. Is that creation of Prema Sai also the work of these wondrous hands?

Sometimes, in the middle of a talk, Baba will suddenly begin clapping his hands, swaying gracefully back and forth to his own rhythmic beat. Typically he will say, "Like you clap your hands to chase away the birds that sit in the tree in your courtyard and foul everything with their droppings, you must also clap your hands, repeating 'Rama, Rama' (Baba's mantra is Sai Ram) to chase away the birds of greed, lust, and envy that sit in the tree of life and foul your own mind."

One of Baba's greatest characteristics is his sense of humor. It is common for him, in the middle of a learned discourse, to suddenly crack a joke or tell an amusing anecdote that has everyone laughing heartily. The central issue of Baba's talks, the *sine qua non* of his teaching, what it is all aimed at, though expressed in a thousand different ways, is our transformation. As he says himself, "I don't want your praise. I want your transformation." We have to begin with ourselves and correct our own defects if we want a better world. There is no other way. It is an illusion to think that the world will change as we all want it to do, if we ourselves do not change.

I once heard an American devotee say, "You would be a fool if you do not see Baba's divinity." You would indeed be blind. There are, however, many who do not want to change, and they are unable to see Baba's divinity. The decision is entirely, and quite properly, theirs, and they are allowed the free will to make it. But for those who want something better, something higher than being tied down to a petty ego, who want to uncover their real self, who want to achieve unity with the divine and their fellow beings, a thorough cleaning of their human nature is indispensable. Baba tells us, "Your heart can become Vaikunta if you but purify it and allow God to manifest in it." Vaikunta means "the place where there is no shadow of grief." "When God manifests in your heart all is full and free." It is through Baba's grace that this difficult goal can be achieved, but according to him, we have to work hard to win that grace.

The evening talks at Whitefield always conclude with bhajans, although if it is late, only one or two are sung. Once Baba has left the hall, I have often seen Western men, who otherwise would not normally demonstrate their feelings, bow down reverently at Baba's footstool. There is no doubt that life in the West today is a mad rat race and Westerners who visit Baba are often in a state of great stress. As a result, when they sit at the divine's feet in an atmosphere charged with divine compassion, the relief they feel is often so great that this spontaneous act can only be seen as an expression of their gratitude. In India people take life at a more leisurely pace. Eternity is theirs! Others who come to scoff may remain to pray. Such is the power of this great godhead.

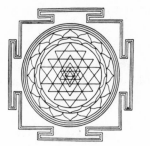

Puri

On my return to India from a trip to Denmark, I made yet another stopover in a holy city, this time Puri, considered one of the holiest cities in India. It is situated south of Calcutta, on the Bay of Bengal, and I found there further proof of Baba's fame. Whenever I mentioned I was a Sai devotee, I was treated with great respect. "Oh, Baba," people would say, "He is God." Puri is a very religious town.

The great attraction in Puri is the temple of Lord Jaganath (Lord of the Universe, another name for the Divine). I was eager to see it, but when I arrived I was told that foreigners are not permitted to enter the temple. An immense and noisy crowd milled around in the big square in front of the temple. As I stood, transfixed, looking at the temple, a cold, clammy hand suddenly gripped mine and a man's voice whispered in my ear, "Come with me." I quickly freed my hand from the unpleasant grasp and followed the man to a three-storied building situated right opposite the temple.

I followed my guide up a long, dark, narrow, and dirty staircase to a terrace that had a marvelous view over the huge and ancient temple. It was built in the 12th century and is regarded as one of India's most magnificent monuments. The temple is the highest temple in Orissa and can be seen for many kilometers around. It is reputed to have one of the world's largest kitchens, subdivided into 452 smaller kitchens, that serve *mahaprasad* (sacred food) everyday to thousands of devotees.

Puri is also a seaside resort, relatively undiscovered by tourists. The sunny beach is one of the finest in the world and stretches for kilometers along a nonpolluted ocean front. The sunrise there is a kaleidoscope of colors, and is a magnificent experience.

While in Puri, I also visited the Karar ashram where Paramahansa Yogananda was initiated into Kriya Yoga by his beloved master, Sri Yukteswar. Today the ashram is presided over by another Paramahansa, Swami Hariharananda, a great master who is known all over India and has initiated thousands of people in Kriya Yoga. His devotees say he opens the wide horizons of the spirit and grants inner peace to those who come in contact with him. Swami Hariharananda is now in his 80s and spends most of his time in New York. Indeed, he was away in New York when I first visited Puri, but later I was to have a profound spiritual experience in his presence.

Life without
a Spiritual Ballast
Is Not Worth Living

I returned to my own Lord Jaganath (Baba) in Puttaparthi after a short encounter with western culture in Denmark that convinced me more than ever that life without a spiritual ballast is not worth living. It seemed a purely mechanical existence, an insane race to fit into "the system," and thereby to be isolated in a prison of our own making, which frequently leads to a variety of neuroses. But there is a remedy— opt out, get the ego out of the way and let the divine take the lead. Much humility is needed if we are to find our own true inner self. The following stories illustrate how Baba knows at all times what befalls us and how he acts in his own mysterious way, in his own time.

Two men decided to go to Puttaparthi for the first time to visit Baba. One was a professor at a scientific institute in Bangalore. They elected to make the journey by train. While on the train, the professor attempted to open a window in their compartment. As he did so the window slammed down on his thumb causing a painful injury. Before long the thumb had swollen to three times its normal size and turned completely black. The pain was so great the professor was unable to sleep that night and began to fear the onset of gangrene. He thought his thumb might even have to be amputated.

The next morning, however, the professor and his friend took their place in the darshan line and awaited the appearance of Swami. As Baba passed where the men were sitting he appeared to ignore them and even seemed to turn his back on them. But as he turned, the seam of his robe brushed over the professor's swollen thumb and almost immediately the painful throbbing stopped. Gradually, during the day, the swelling and black color subsided. By evening that same day, the thumb had returned to normal.

The incident reminded me of a personal experience I had that was also related to a train journey. I was in Delhi and took the train to Hardwar, making sure to book a sleeper for the overnight journey. I shared the compartment with another lady who was accompanied by her husband. A sleeping berth in India, by the way, is a bed and nothing more, no pillow or blankets are supplied.

When the lady went to bed, her husband produced a padded quilt which he placed over her, before leaving the compartment for the night. I thought to myself, "We're hardly traveling in an arctic climate." We had left Delhi in oppressive heat, and I could barely refrain from laughing at the sight of my fellow passenger lying buried under a quilt with only the tip of her nose visible. In contrast, I was wearing only a thin summer dress.

My amusement didn't last long. As the train traveled further and further north, the temperature dropped to below zero. Never in my life have I frozen as I did that night. I was trembling like a leaf when I left the train at Hardwar next morning, where the ground was covered with white frost. As a result, I caught an ailment that took years to get over.

In fact, it was not until I discovered Baba that the complaint finally left me. One morning, as I was sitting in darshan line within the mandir compound at Prasanthi Nilayam, feeling particularly unhappy about my difficulty, Baba showed that he knew all about it. In his usual, unpretentious way he came out of the temple and casually asked one of the students seated on the verandah for a sheet of paper. The boy quickly tore a page from his notebook and handed it to Baba. With the paper in his hand Baba walked to the edge of the verandah and stood facing toward where I was sitting in the darshan line. Keeping me squarely in his gaze, he slowly began tearing the paper into smaller and smaller pieces until there was nothing left of it. I presume that none of the more than one thousand other devotees seated in the temple compound that day had any idea what was happening. But I understood what it meant. That morning I was rid of the ailment that had plagued me for several years, and it has never returned since. Who can fathom his ways?

These examples certainly don't mean that Baba cures all and sundry who come to him with illnesses. For instance, if an evil person who was unwell, but otherwise did not want to change, was suddenly cured by Baba, he might become even more wicked, once he recovered. Such a cure would have no meaning. Only the divine knows when it is the right time for a cure.

But it is not to cure people's ailments that Baba is here — that is only a side issue. He is here to awaken us to our true birthright, the rediscovery of our true selves. When that has been found, life is filled with such joy, peace, and serenity that our health automatically improves, for then we are living in harmony with ourselves and the order of the universe.

A Pilgrimage

I decided to make Puri, the famous place of pilgrimage, my destination once again. Each day hundreds of pilgrims visit its famous Lord Jaganath Temple. At festival times the numbers swell to thousands. But my trip this time was to visit the small, but beautiful Karar Ashram. It is one of the focal points in the world for the study of Kriya yoga, although only monks are permitted to live there. Kriya promises much and its devotees say, "By the practice of Kriya you attain God realization, which is self-realization, at rocket speed." I had asked for, and received Baba's blessings before I began my journey, and I half expected to return to him as an enlightened person.

I wanted to learn the Kriya yoga exercises from Swami Hariharananda Giri himself. At that time he presided over the ashram, although he usually only spent a couple of weeks a year there. He usually spent a good deal of his time in America and as much as nine months a year traveled in other foreign countries. As Swami Hariharananda said, "These countries have everything except peace. The people are in frustration, sorrow, and trouble." Slowly he was helping them to "get calmness, which is Godliness."

Swami Hariharananda Giri usually returned to Puri each year on the founder day of the Karar Ashram (March 22), and thus this particular year (1989), he arrived in mid-March from New York via Calcutta by the Jaganath Express to Puri.

The ashram was founded by Swami Sri Yukteswar Giri, the guru of Paramahansa Yogananda who wrote the famous book, *The Autobiography of a Yogi*. Swami Hariharananda is considered to be the greatest living master-saint of the scientific technique of Kriya yoga, and occupies a high rank among the Indian yogis of this century.

Shortly after his arrival, he gave darshan to the many people waiting for him at the ashram, and afterward some were invited to his room. I was fortunate enough to be among them, and it was, in itself, a great experience to sit in the presence of this saint. He exchanged a few words with many of the group. To me he said, "You ought to feel transformation by seeing me." And indeed I did. My whole being was enveloped in a soothing peace. I told Swami Hariharananda that I was a devotee of Sri Sathya Sai Baba. In the meditation hall at the Karar Ashram are pictures of Sai Baba, Shirdi Baba, Sri Aurobindo, and the Mother.

Suddenly a young man entered Swami Hariharananda's room, made his way quickly through all of us who were sitting cross-legged on the carpeted floor, and went straight up to the saint and knelt in front of him. The Swami embraced him warmly several times, apparently very happy to see him. After about half-an-hour Swami Hariharananda indicated that he wished people to leave the room so that he could rest after his long journey.

It is not possible to stay at the Karar ashram, so I checked into one of the many beachside hotels along the coast, many of which are reasonably priced. My small hotel was situated almost on the beach itself, and I was able to swim in the ocean several times a day.

During his short stay, Swami Hariharananda seemed very busy and allowed himself very little time for rest. I marveled at how someone well over 80 could sustain all the activity. More and more people arrived every day, many from foreign countries, until there were at least six to seven hundred devotees who were present to receive his blessings.

About two hundred were initiated in Kriya yoga by the Swami. For everyone else it seemed a very hard program, but he remained peaceful and calm, the very embodiment of the Kriya he was teaching. I noticed that often in the ashram's big hall he asked devotees not to do *padnamaskar* as he left. "Don't bow, don't bow," he said repeatedly.

After a few days he sent for me. A meeting had been arranged for 11:00 A.M. of the appointed day, but I experienced great difficulty reaching the ashram. Unknown to me, that particular day was a festival day called "Holi" during which children and young people are permitted to spray or smear colored dyes on all and sundry. I left my hotel with time to spare and dressed in good clothes, but being a foreigner with a pale skin, I was soon a favorite target. Before I was halfway to the ashram, my face was green and the rest of me was the colors of the rainbow. I felt I couldn't appear before the Swami looking like that and hurried back to my hotel to wash and change. For my second attempt I wore a rain coat and wrapped my face in a towel!

I finally reached the ashram and a secretary showed me into Swami Hariharananda's room. As I entered, my eyes went immediately to his silent figure sitting in an unassuming position on a cot covered with an orange cloth. There was no one else in the room. I went to where he was sitting and knelt down in front of him. There was no small talk or exchange of social niceties. His first, very direct question was, "Why have you come?" I answered, truthfully, that I understood Kriya to be a scientific and universal technique and a short cut to a higher dimension of consciousness, which I wanted to reach. I added that, as such, I did not see any difficulty combining Kriya with *bhakti* (devotion) to my own master, Sri Sathya Sai Baba.

Swami Hariharananda did not reply to this. Without further questions he rose and bolted the door from the inside to ensure there were no interruptions, then sat down on the floor next to me. "Give me a shirt," he asked. I rose and attempted to hand him one of the shirts hanging on a string in the spartan and simple room. But the shirt I selected had long sleeves and he said, "No, not that one." Instead I handed him a short-sleeved shirt, which he pulled over his head with the simplicity of a child. All the while his whole attitude reflected the command of a yogi who is above it all. I sat down again next to him on the floor, feeling quite relaxed and almost at home in his room.

Swami Hariharananda then said, "I will perform a purification of your body." With his hand he touched the different chakras in my spine, one by one. He then held my hands firmly in his hands. He even held my feet in his hands. Then he used one hand to stroke my face, arms, and back, all the while repeating Vedic mantras in Sanskrit. In English he said, "I am infusing my life force in you."

During this purification process I saw a dazzling white light in the position of the so-called "third eye" between the eyebrows. According to Swami Hariharananda, that white light is the light of the soul. I also clearly heard the cosmic OM sound that underlies creation. Finally he put his hand on my head and blessed me, and I bent down and touched his feet.

It was such an overwhelming experience that I had difficulty holding back the tears that had started to form under my closed eyelids. It had all taken place in five minutes and throughout I had invoked Baba as Ista (God). Almost immediately I experienced an extreme calmness that remained with me for the rest of that day. It was so great that it was impossible to come down to that plane where we make ordinary conversation. The 'I' and the 'me' had disappeared. I observed silence for the rest of the day, letting the blessed peace envelope my whole being. It felt as if I were staying at the center of my being. The aim of Kriya yoga, and indeed all yoga, is to go into that center and remain there and realize the self.

Paramahansa Hariharananda wants you to find "the real chamber of your being and to enjoy the world like a king, not like a beggar." He says, "The helplessness in you, which has made you a beggar, disappears and you find an unshakable shelter in your own self." Here are a few examples of his teachings:

Love bears.
Love tolerates.
Love is not resentful.
Love requires patience.
Love gives oneness.
Love is kind.
Love is sweet.
Love is God, without God there is no love.

So long as you have not cleaned your heart nicely, you cannot do anything nicely. You cannot love. So you are to clean your heart and to clean your mind.

Heaven and hell are within you. Verbally you are very sweet, but inwardly bitter, sugarcoated quinine. But remember, you are the power of God.

Meditate. Watch day and night. Constant alertness in every step of your life is necessary. Then you will have quickest result.

Make your life a divine life, not a devil's life. If you have anger, pride, ego and hatred, then eradicate all these devil's qualities.

You are the power of God. Feel it in your practical life. Perceive the Ultimate Truth. Be calm and be divine. Get up from your body sense and worldly sense. You need culture. If you want to meditate, you are to go beyond mind, thought, intellect, restlessness, anger, etc.

God wants that you should transform yourself. God is giving you constant blows for your correction. But you are not following Him.

Meditation is the way to self-discovery. To know truth we have to go deeper. There is only one method of acquiring knowledge. From the ordinary person to the highest yogi — all have to use the same method, and that method is concentration. This is the knock that opens the gates of nature and lets out floods of light. Concentration is the only key to the treasure of knowledge. The power of the human mind is unlimited. The secret of the world is ours, if we know how to knock, how to give the necessary blow. The strength and force of the blow come through concentration.

By remaining in the superconscious state, a yogi gets extreme love, regard and indebtedness to God. This love for God is very rare.

However insignificant a thing may be, it is He. But if you do not meditate very deeply, you can not perceive this truth.

Those who have penetrated into the veils of nature's creation, those who have realized the truth of all religions, those who are free from anger, emotion, hallucination, speculation are the real teachers.

Returning to Sai Baba's ashram at Puttaparthi, I felt that this experience had deepened my love for Baba and that through it I had come closer to him and learned that in the world of today his divinity is unparalleled.

Oh, precious Lord of my heart.
You made me see my soul in all its glory.
You made me hear the cosmic sound of OM from deep
within.
You are Ista, indeed one with all creation.
A thousand times I bow down to Thee.

That Which Holds
the Great Subcontinent
of India Together

On the way back from Puri, a friend and I broke our journey at Hyderabad to visit the Sai Baba temple and the Venketeshwara temple in the nearby hills. The whole trip had given me a deeper insight into the ancient culture of India. I became aware that if anything is to save the world from its present crises, including India (for modern India has forgotten her heritage) then it is this wonderful ancient culture.

The one thing that has held the great sub-continent of India together from the earliest times—despite its people speaking different languages in different regions, despite differences in habits and modes of life—is a basic faith and belief in the One of a Thousand Forms, who is yet the same Absolute. That belief has such deep roots all over the country that wherever you go, you find the same fundamentals. But these days many of them have taken on a rigid, external form. Many Indians seem too bound up in traditions whose origins lie in caste, myth, and ritual. Often they put their faith in the stars. Did the great Vivekananda not say, "Do not put your faith in planets and stars. If a star disturbs my life it is not worth a cent. To be tricked by twinkling stars is a shameful condition."

Sri Sathya Sai Baba is here, however, to awaken the people of this sacred country to its true genius, that of the spirit, without which all the rest is nothing. And when that awakening happens, its impulse will spread universally and it will hold the whole world together.

The countless temples in India bear witness to its deep religious spirit. There are seven sacred mountains in India. The Himalayas in the north are the tallest and loftiest in the world, and extend from the eastern to the western oceans. One of the lesser known mountains is Neeladri, outside Hyderabad. Here, perched on the top, is the white marble Venketeshwara temple. It was built in modern times and its beauty is indescribable.

Into the walls of the entire complex — which has many floors up along the hillside and numerous big halls — are cut, in white marble, scenes from the rich history of India, such as the Bhagavad Gita — Lord Krishna as the charioteer of Arjuna during the great battle of Kurukshetra. The stairs to the temple are guarded by two mighty lions sculptured from white marble. The whole temple is a masterpiece of art and composition. People come from near and far to see it, and it is said to be one of the wealthiest temples of the world. My friend and I, of course, also wanted to see the Sri Sathya Sai Baba temple in Hyderabad. There are Sai Baba temples in Bombay, Hyderabad, and Madras and they are called, respectively, Sathyam (truth), Shivam (auspiciousness), and Sundaram (beauty).

Because of our flight time to Bangalore, we only had half-an-hour to spend in the beautiful temple. Its outstanding feature is the unique dome formed like a *lingam* (an oval, egg-shape) which is the symbol of Shiva, as well as of creation. Sai Baba sometimes creates a lingam from the five elements for a devotee who needs it. They are extremely beautiful and are often intended for healing. The day before our visit to the temple, Baba had stopped there for three hours on his way back from Madras. Its atmosphere was still filled with the sweetness of his presence. This atmosphere cannot be found in any other temple in the world, however grandiose it may be.

After our short, but refreshing stay in the Shivam temple, we drove to the airport to catch our plane. Soon we were back in the physical presence of Baba. Swami is a magnet with an irresistible force of attraction for all seekers of Truth.

Taste the Truth

Before I left Puri I asked Swami Hariharananda if he would initiate me into Kriya yoga. He answered with just one word, "No," and that was that. He also called me "a baby" and told me I could not follow two masters, although that was never my intention. "You have been here in India for so long," he said, "and you haven't seen God yet." It was quite a reprimand.

To see God in yourself, which is what the Swami meant, is not such a simple affair. Sai Baba is God, which this saint surely acknowledged. To know intuitively Sai Baba as God is one thing, but to know myself as God is quite another and infinitely more difficult. Baba, though, has assured me any number of times, "I am God, but you also are God. The only difference between us is that I know it and you do not."

I learned later that in a proper initiation into Kriya the aspirant goes through quite a ceremony in which he or she promises obedience to the Kriya Masters. They are very high beings, and some of them are even said to have been avatars. The aspirant must also promise to keep the Kriya technique itself a secret, partly to prevent it from being abused and because to talk carelessly about it dissipates the accumulated energy. The ceremony often takes between one or two hours, during which rituals are performed and candles, lights, and flowers offered to the master. The Swami in Puri certainly gives the perception of divinity and once a disciple has been initiated, Swami takes responsibility for him or her until that person reaches liberation. When I learned all this I, without a moments hesitation, dropped the whole idea of Kriya. I left it at the wayside, as it were, as I left Puri.

Between a *sishya* (aspiring disciple) and her Lord is an unbreakable bond of love, and when I returned to Baba he showed me I had been on the wrong track. His teachings follow another path. In Kriya the aspirant goes through quite a vigorous discipline in order to open the six centers, or chakras of the subtle nervous system in the spine. It is a scientific method that seems to work along tantric lines and aims at awakening what is called the Kundalini shakti lying dormant and coiled up at the base of the spine. There is no doubt that it is a very powerful method, so much so that the guidance of a guru who has himself practiced this opening of the centers and become *siddha* (one who has attained self-realization) is indispensable.

Sri Aurobindo said, "The Kundalini is also above us, above our heads as the divine force—not there coiled up—involved; asleep—but awake, scient, potent, extended and wide."[7] This force is Baba's *shakti* (creative power). He is in full command of it, as he has so abundantly proved. According to the Indian scriptures, the very definition of an avatar is that he manifests God consciousness and its divine power (*shakti*) in a human mind.

In Baba's yoga it is not necessary to go through a systematized method, actually there is no method at all. There is no attempt to open the chakras. The whole aim of his teachings is to raise the consciousness to higher levels or, in his own words, to "re-establish dharma (righteousness)," which amounts to the same thing. When this happens, the chakras open by themselves, often without us being aware of it.

Lord Krishna, in the Bhagavad Gita, said, "Whensoever there is the fading of the dharma and the uprising of unrigh-

---

[7]Sri Aurobindo, *Letters on Yoga, Vol. 3*, p. 1150.

teousness then I loose myself forth into birth, for the deliverance of the good, for the destruction of evil-doers, for the enthroning of the Right." If there was ever such a time, it is now. And this is Baba's mission, as he himself maintains. His divine force is acting not only upon the individual but also upon the world resulting in a general upliftment of consciousness. He gives us a dharma, a law of self-discipline, by which to grow out of the lower into the higher life. This is what is taking place today among his devotees, especially among his students.

According to the Vedas, we are all projected from a common center — God — and we all have to return to this center. Baba is taking us back to this point, or as far along the path as we can follow him. He has the power to do so for he is one with our soul. He is the divine, he is at the center of our being.

For our part, we must work hard to win his grace. We have to be entirely sincere, sincerity is the valid passport for his divine shakti to enter us and do its work. But is it a sign of sincerity to talk incessantly and immediately after his darshan, as many do? How can his shakti work in us in such circumstances? We ourselves, by our thoughtless behavior, have closed the door for its passage. What a shame it is to risk spoiling the unique chance we have been given to absorb the divinity he pours over us, which enables us to change. It is the only thing he asks of us.

If we keep the door open, a look is often the means he uses to transmit his shakti to us. You can reach a point where you feel shakti physically enter your soul. To me, the most natural place for it to enter is the heart-center, or chakra, as that center is the true abode of the Lord. There are six centers of the subtle body that envelope the gross body, but living at the level of ordinary consciousness we are not aware of them. Each center is symbolized by a lotus with a certain number of petals, beginning with four petals for the lowest center. A Kriya disciple, for example, would work very hard to get the heart-center to open and have its twelve lotus petals lift upward, instead of drooping down as they would in ordinary consciousness.

This heart-center becomes extremely alive when the divine enters. Intense vibrations of sweetness and peace emanate from it and penetrate the whole being, almost like an intoxicating wine. It is the highest good for a devotee to be alone with the divine in that chamber. And to achieve this, it is not necessary to go into seclusion, or do Kriya. It is just as likely to be experienced in a crowded bus, spilling over with passengers as is the custom in India. Suddenly the Presence is there. It is felt like a deep calmness, an inner warmth, there is a sense of freedom, and above all perhaps, of absolute security. You embrace the whole world with a smile. In that state of consciousness, you automatically do the right thing at the right time, moving forward through life with much greater surety and efficiency.

You can also attract his shakti by calling persistently to the divine, "Swami come to me, please," trying ardently to tune into his wavelength, and he will come. Your whole being is then lifted by his presence. You feel detachment in a world of attachments. To taste the truth of it, you must experience it yourself. It is such a blessed state you find yourself praying, again and again, "Stay with me, Swami." But he never does. I presume this is probably because the inner consciousness is not developed sufficiently to hold onto that elevated state of mind, which is so very different from ordinary consciousness.

Another "technique" is to do *namasmarana* (constant repetition and reflection on the name of the Lord). It is not easy to always repeat the Lord's name, but if it is done with feeling and not just parrot fashion, it is a very powerful means to the same end. There are many ways to win Swami's grace—in recent years Baba has placed great emphasis on selfless service to others in the community.

The Kriya Master in Puri was right, then, when he called me "a baby." What he meant was why come to him who was surely a great master, when I in fact lived at the feet of an avatar. Why go through unnecessary trouble, when just a look from the Divine can and does have the same result as perhaps many years of Kriya.

"My life is my message," Baba says and that message, first and foremost, is his *Prema* (love). It is such a formidable power, and his sole weapon against the so-called *asuric* (hostile) forces, of which the world is so full. They cannot come near him. They do not dare. But he also wards them away from a sincere devotee so that he or she is protected.

There is an epilogue to my adventure with Kriya yoga. After my return from Puri, I wrote in a letter to Swami that I thought, for me, Kriya had been a "complete mistake." In fact I wrote two letters, more or less in the same vein, and Swami took them both. He wanted to teach me a lesson. Both letters were returned, but not until about a month later, when Swami had returned from a trip to the mountains. He knew of course what was in the letters. Both were sent back in the same way Swami had once sent me flowers, only this time I received an admonition, not flowers.

One evening, as I was about to go to bhajans at Whitefield, I found the two letters stuck between the double doors of my flat. The sight of them gave me quite a shock. Knowing Swami's ways, I felt I already knew how they got there. But to make sure, I asked my neighbor, who usually sat outside watching her children, if anyone had delivered mail. She assured me there hadn't been anybody.

The incident occurred on May 27, which to me was significant. As most Sai devotees know, the Divine's number is 9; and three 9s make 27. I believe the lesson he wanted to teach me was that I should show more respect for his alternative, yet nonetheless great system of yoga. It was not a lesson that I would easily forget, and I ought to have known better. Once before when I had ventured a critical remark on something of far less importance, Swami had turned his back on me in a very demonstrative way. This time it was much more serious.

It should be noted that it was not a question of Swami carrying my letters around with him for a month while he toured in the mountains. Baba receives hundreds of letters every day, and when he is finished with them, each day they are burned. Clearly he must have materialized them, in his usual style, in order for them to be returned. The first letter was unopened, in the envelope in which it had been given to Swami. The other letter had just been written on a page of paper and there it was fluttering in the breeze. It even had the same wrong date I had mistakenly put on it, which I recalled being annoyed about after I had handed the letter to Swami. I was flabbergasted, to say the least.

Just a few minutes after I had discovered my letters in the door, I met Swami himself, just coming out of his house. Involuntarily I did *namaskar* (holding the palms together on the chest) and said, "Thank you, Swami." He looked at me in his direct way, and somehow I felt that his leela in returning the letters was also meant as confirmation that my home was at his feet. Later he was to give me an experience equally as profound as the one I had undergone in Puri.

A Delightful Morning with Sai at the Hill View Stadium

Narayana Seva Day (service of God) is a traditional day in India for feeding the poor. At Prasanthi Nilayam, the day usually precedes the celebration of the Hindu *Dasara* festival (the victory of the forces of light over the forces of darkness). It takes place in the huge, open air Hill View Stadium, which is about twelve hundred fifty feet long and about six hundred and fifty feet wide, with the capacity to seat half a million people. The western boundary of the stadium is a rocky cliff, about one hundred and fifty feet high, painted with short sayings from Baba's teachings such as: "Life is a journey from I to we." "Faith is beyond reason." "An evil eye sees evil in others." "Slander is the worst sin."

On a plateau in the cliff itself is an impressive, forty-foot statue of Jesus Christ showering his love and grace in a way that is reminiscent of the Sermon on the Mount. A little further away stands a lovely, twenty-five-foot statue of Zarathustra and to its right a magnificent twenty-foot statue of Lord Shiva sitting in a lotus position looking solemn and majestic. On a terraced platform higher up the cliff is a charming twenty-five-foot statue of Lord Krishna playing his flute.

At one end of the stadium, on the southeast border, is the *Shanti Vedica* (the seat of peace) containing a massive stage, about sixty feet wide, forty feet deep, and seventy feet high. From here Baba gives darshan, delivers discourses, and presides over a variety of displays, celebrations, and festivals. There is a large painting on the back wall of the stage depicting the famous battle at Kurukshetra when Arjuna, aided by Krishna, overcame the forces of King Dhritarashtra. This legendary clash between the pious Pandava brothers and their malevolent cousins, the Kauravas, is described in the Bhagavad Gita and symbolizes the triumph of good over evil. The stage is built in an oriental style, with the roof richly decorated in the fashion of an ancient Indian temple. To the east of the stadium are three large triple-storied buildings, comprising a student hostel, a primary and high school, and a sports center used by Baba's college students.

On this particular Narayana Seva Day about fifteen thousand people attended. The poor are truly rich in the sense that they received the Divine's grace so abundantly. Today they were to be clothed and fed by the Lord himself. These peasant people in India are close to nature and are unspoiled and uncontaminated by the atmosphere of big cities. There had been a heavy downpour overnight and organizers were worried about how to seat so many people, most of whom had walked for hours from neighboring villages, on the rain sodden ground. But, to everyone's surprise, in the morning the sun was shining on perfectly smooth, dry ground.

Mr. Narasimhan, editor of *Sanathana Sarathi* (the monthly ashram magazine that has been published since 1958), spoke about the incident that evening in the Poornachandra Hall. In an opening address, before Baba gave a talk, he said he considered it to be one of Baba's leelas and had suggested to Baba that his leelas be published in *Sanathana Sarathi*. But Swami had answered, "Not even all the volumes of *Sanathana Sarathi* can contain all my leelas."

As part of the massive operation to offer help to the 15,000 poor gathered in the Hill View Stadium, a big truck arrived loaded with bales of clothing, dhotis and shirts for the men and saris for the ladies. There was an expectant hush as everyone waited for the divine himself. As the Sai College students sang bhajans, Swami was driven up in his car. He smiled as he walked through the huge crowd of men, women, and children. Straight away he began distributing clothing. Some recipients showed their gratitude with tears, others held both hands, with palms together, above their heads as a mark of respect. Many in the crowd were dressed in the well-worn clothes they received from Swami the previous year and clearly this was their once a year opportunity to obtain new clothing.

Each person in the vast crowd was also served a full meal, waited upon by college students ferrying food from huge pots. The food had been cooking from early morning in makeshift kitchens set up especially for this occasion. The atmosphere was charged with divinity.

On some festival occasions even greater crowds assemble in the stadium grounds, and even the surrounding cliffs are packed with people. One such time is clearly etched in my memory. It was an international rally of 5,000 Bal Vikas children who had traveled to Puttaparthi from all over the world, accompanied by their teachers. In the morning there was a parade, music and festivities. The first item on the evening program, a dance drama by a solo dancer, held the big audience spellbound. It was followed by an interesting film, *Cosmic Play*, projected on a huge screen and showing the movements of celestial bodies around the sun. At the same time, these movements were duplicated in a live performance by dancers on the stage.

It was a dark evening, with few stars in the sky, and the stage was brilliantly lit by a number of projectors casting a variety of colors. First the planet Mars came on the scene, bathed in red lights, with just two small feet showing under the planet. In the same manner, came Jupiter, followed by the Moon with all its craters painted on the surface. Eventually all the planets emerged and danced a beautiful, harmonious dance. Not once did they collide, a lesson to us all, perhaps, to attempt to live together in harmony. Suddenly all the lights were switched off and in the pitch black the Bal Vikas children swarmed in on stage. Each one held a light, symbolizing the twinkling stars in the firmament and in the dark of the night all attention was focused on those stars.

The whole play was a delight to watch and ended with the divine himself making his way on stage to take part by boarding a "spacecraft." Luckily it was a model, unable to transport him away into space, or there would have been tears instead of the enthusiastic applause that greeted him. The celestial atmosphere of that evening, free and fresh, entered everyone's hearts as they made their way home.

On the eastern border of the Hill View Stadium, this wonderful meeting place for the huge Sai family, is yet another stage, used mostly for dance performances. During the week-long international Bal Vikas conference, it was the setting for a number of excellent dance dramas from all the different regions of India. All displayed great variety of character and were beautifully executed. And always the divine was the main guest and attraction.

These days it is rare to see such superb dance performances anywhere in the world. After an evening watching these classical Indian dances, one young man, with a keen eye for beauty, remarked spontaneously, "They can't do it better on Broadway."

Whenever the divine is present there is always beauty. Everyone feels blessed on such occasions—to watch the divine drama of Lord Rama (an avatar of God, the source of all joy, delight, bliss).

"God is Love and Love is God"

"God is love and love is God," says Baba. But what is love? Love is a word that is hopelessly misused and misunderstood. Does not love basically signify a need of some kind, your love of this person or that thing to satisfy your need? The love between man and woman satisfies the need, each for the other, whether it be physical, or companionship, or comfort, or another need. If there is no longer any need, love can turn to indifference, perhaps even hatred. Why do people, married or otherwise, change partners so often, particularly in the West? For the simple reason, I think, that they no longer seem to satisfy each other's particular needs.

God's love has nothing to do with this worldly concept of love—love which always expects something in return for what is given. God's love is love for love's sake. It is without the slightest trace of self-interest. It is unconditional; it can also be cold as ice. This can occur, whether consciously or unconsciously, when our ego gives us an inflated sense of our importance, then God's love freezes. "God's love," it has been said, "can be conceived only as a state of fullness, wholeness, holiness—no words can be adequate. It is the very soul of the entire universe."

Such love is manifested today here on earth as it was in the days of Christ, but now this love is supported by a tremendous power and dynamism. It penetrates all that comes in contact with it. It changes ugliness to beauty, darkness to light, ignorance to knowledge, selfishness to goodness, and awakens in every being the awareness of God's presence. Baba could be adequately described as "the Hope of Humanity." He is initiating a new world order, and this is done solely by the majesty of the love that flows from him.

Baba says, "The whole world is bleeding because of its lovelessness. Today, scientists and leaders of nations have forgotten the true values of life and the real good of the world. They are obsessed only with material progress. Unless they are awakened to the spiritual values of life, there cannot be any peace and prosperity in the world. Without spiritual bases, even if people have eyes they are blind, even if they have ears they are deaf, even if intellectually brilliant they are insane. Spirituality alone confers true vision and makes us full and wholesome."

At a time when the whole of humankind is groaning under the deepest psychological crises humanity has ever known, the highest godhead has descended upon earth to help us out of it. The darkness is always deepest before dawn, but dawn is breaking. Baba is transforming humankind into its best all over the globe. Let us open the inner closed doors to the light that is descending. Then there will be plentitude, dharma, greatness, variety, and strength—for that is his will. The whole of humanity is waiting for this hour.

Dasara

Baba, being the Supreme Harmonizer and the avatar who has come to revive the Vedas and the traditions of *Sanathana Dharma* (the ancient wisdom; the eternal path), directs the magnificent Dasara festival each September at Prasanthi Nilayam. Dasara celebrates the victory of the forces of good over the forces that resist the progress of humans toward light. The festival lasts nine days, with a tenth day reserved for a special purification ceremony performed by Baba. Seven days are devoted to the adoration of the feminine aspects of the divine personality, whose might and majesty are glorified in the Vedas.

Throughout the festival, the Vedas are chanted to promote the welfare and prosperity of the world. This is done in the beautiful Poornachandra hall by specially invited, learned pundits who wear picturesque orange silk robes and cream colored shawls. They are seated on stage around a sacred fire, which is kept burning for the duration of the festival. Dry sticks and wood are constantly added to the fire and ceremonially fed with *ghee*, a clarified butter. Loudspeakers are erected so that the continual chanting of hymns and mantras can be heard all over the ashram.

Each evening throughout the seven days Baba gives a discourse. The basic refrain of these powerful talks may be summed up in two words: "transform yourselves." In other words, if people do not change themselves, how can they expect the world to change?

Before Baba's talks on some evenings during the Dasara festival, one or two students speak about their experiences of school life with the divine himself as their chancellor. He looks after them with all the care of a mother, but they say, he can also be very stern with students when it is for their own good. He wants no impurities, no obstacles, no defects to hinder the harmonious development of hand, head, and heart.

Baba wants excellence from his students and puts special stress on character building, and character means efficiency to the core. "I want quality not quantity," he says. It is a unique privilege for these young students to grow up under his loving care, and they all adore him. The best proof of this is that during holidays more than half of them stay in their colleges to be together with Baba, instead of going home to their parents.

One evening during a recent Dasara, a student told about an interesting incident. Baba had gone out for a long drive. A devotee was driving the car at a good speed, when suddenly he saw a snake on the road directly in front of the car. He didn't know what to do. He was going too quickly to slam on the brakes, or to try and swerve around it, without running the car off the road. He quickly glanced at Baba in the back seat and saw he had his eyes closed. At the last moment, he decided to drive on, right over the snake. When they returned to Prasanthi Nilayam in the evening, the devotee was anxious to know if Baba had noticed the incident and whether he would mention it. But Baba got out of the car without saying anything. The next morning at darshan, as Baba came near the man who had been driving the car, he turned his back. The devotee was stunned when he saw on Baba's back the outline of a snake lying under two wheel tracks. It indicated clearly not only that Baba knew about the incident, but proved his own statement that he is one with all creation. I presume that the unfortunate creature was given a painless passage. The story also demonstrates a little of Baba's *Prema* (love) which expressed itself very early in his life when, as a small boy, he saw a chicken about to be slaughtered. He immediately grasped it and hugged it to his chest thus saving its life.

After one of Baba's evening discourses, Bal Vikas children presented a colorful dance drama with appropriate settings and music. The platform looked almost like some heavenly abode because of an artistic floral background using a wide range of auspicious flowers. Two huge peacocks were gracefully depicted at the entrance to *Vaikunta* (Heaven) — all done in flowers.

On another evening, there was a symbolic representation of the national unity brought about by Swami in the Sathya Sai colleges and institutions — where his students live in great harmony. Students expressed their feelings regarding Swami's majestic form, his glorious mission, and the close relationship they all have with him in poems and song. Simultaneously, shadow dances were projected onto a screen at the back of the stage. It was a simple and sincere tribute, lovingly and charmingly done. At the end of the play, a flock of white doves was released and flew out over the heads of the audience.

The final day was the highlight of the festival. Baba walked from the mandir to the Poornachandra Hall in a procession led by Sai Gita, his pet elephant. She had been bathed for the occasion and had Indian designs painted on her large forehead and a gold embroidered cloth on her back. A large brass bell hung from her neck. Sai Gita was followed by a score of students chanting Vedic hymns and over thirty pundits in their orange silk robes and cream colored shawls. In the middle of all this walked Sathya Sai Baba. Drummers beat out a fanfare as he entered the hall and twenty thousand people massed inside began singing bhajans. Then Baba delivered his dynamic Dasara message on love.

He began by singing these lines in his heart-stirring voice, "You may be enjoying every comfort that wealth and power can give, or you may be suffering the blessings of the goddess of poverty. Whoever you are, whatever you do, if you do not have love in your heart your life is virtually useless. Even if you are the emperor of all emperors, without love you are lower than the lowest servant."

Swami continued, "Love is your real nature and it is your duty to express what is already inherent in you. Every one of you has this sacred principle of divinity in your heart. Do not get arrogant or proud. You may be steeped in difficulties, you may be in great pain, but learn from the Pandavas.[8] In spite of all their extreme difficulties and tribulations, they were never prideful or arrogant, their only response was their unwavering faith in the Lord. Do not do anything mechanically, forcefully, or because of jealousy. Serve all. Do everything with love in your heart. There can be no greater blessings than to have the love and Grace of God. No one can know what he will give to one who has earned his grace. God's love is all there is in the world. The basis and truth of everything is divinity.

"All the riches and gold of the world are really nothing, they are only passing clouds, they are impermanent. God alone is permanent. To have God with you, you must do some simple little things: see only good, hear only good, think only good, do only good, think no evil, speak no evil. Don't praise God, he has no need for it, God is pleased only when you treat him as an intimate friend—that is the way you should relate to God. Consider him as your nearest and dearest. Whether in pain or pleasure he is always by your side. He accompanies you birth after birth. God is inside you, and he is also outside you."

---

[8]Five pious brothers who were princes in one of India's ruling dynasties at the time of Krishna. The best known is Arjuna. Their epic battle at Kurukshetra against their egoistic cousins, the Kauravas, is described in the Bhagavad Gita. They were renowned for their faith and righteousness.

When Baba had concluded his strong talk on love, the pundits brought a big silver pot of sacred water into the hall. Baba then took a short-handled Indian straw broom, and, followed by a priest carrying the pot, walked up and down the aisles using the broom to spray showers of sacred water over all. He seemed to enjoy himself immensely and only a few didn't get drops of blessed water sprinkled on them. It was the end of a very beautiful Dasara festival.

There are quite a few festivals each year at Prasanthi Nilayam. All of the festivals were excellent and thoroughly enjoyed by all devotees. But many people are not aware that each festival has a profound inner meaning and purpose. They are designed to reveal the greatness and integrity of the Indian-Aryan culture, so sadly forgotten in India today. There is no other culture in the recorded history of human-kind that teaches such sublime truths as the Aryan culture — that we exist so that we may fulfill ourselves in the Divine; that we may understand who "I" is, and who the Divine is and the relationship between the two.

No finer, fuller, or greater experience can happen to people than to have the curtain of separation withdrawn from the window of the soul so the light of the supreme can illuminate us with understanding. This is the essence of the culture expressed in a few words. It is the culture of the Vedas, the Bhagavad Gita and the ancient scriptures, and it teaches us how to reach the goal of life. Today it is being revived by Sri Sathya Sai Baba and other great seers of India.

It is this culture, not religious dogmas, that provides the background for the teaching at the Sri Sathya Sai colleges. It concentrates on the universal principles of truth, right conduct, peace, love, non-violence, and the unifying influence of tolerance, faith, and service to others. But it does not do so at the expense of academic standards. The colleges are kept up to date with the best equipment available. The name given to this form of teaching is Education In Human Values (EHV) and modern educators, if they ignore it, are making a great mistake.

Too many college graduates leave their institutions with a head full of "book learning" only to discover that they cannot find their way in life because they have never been taught human values. They plunge headlong into wrong relationships, marriages, sexual excess, and the usual array of bad habits that afflict and distract people in the West, and then have to suffer the consequences. And, as is the fashion these days, the more they try to avoid the consequences of their behavior, the longer the trail of wreckage they leave behind, and the more they suffer.

"Know Truth, know thyself, help man protect the right," is at the core of Baba's teachings. He himself is the embodiment of Truth, and from my experience I am certain, no one can touch that Truth and come away unchanged.

A Secret Darshan

The day after a Dasara festival I received from Baba what I call a "secret darshan," an exchange between us that was intensely personal but which went unnoticed by others. I am sure that sooner or later Swami makes everyone feel that they have had a "secret darshan." It is one of his ways of teaching. He is able to make each of us think we are the special, the only one, and in a way we are. It is the art of the avatar.

Although Dasara was over, a large crowd remained the next day for morning darshan, after which Baba left the temple compound and walked over into the adjacent Poorna-chandra Hall. Many people, myself included, stayed sitting where they were waiting for Baba to return. I took out pen and paper and started writing about the delights of the Dasara festival and about half-an-hour later Baba returned. Everyone looked toward the compound entrance, hands raised with palms together, ready to greet him as he re-entered. Because of my position against a low section of the compound wall, I was able to see Baba coming. Just before he entered he slowly turned his head and sent me a long, deep look. A feeling of happiness welled up from deep within me, soft and gentle, and in that moment I caught a glimpse of the overwhelming compassion and tenderness on his face.

A look from Baba has magic power. It can open for you a dimension of your being that you did not know existed. At that moment, nothing existed but the divine. But why, I thought, should he give me this "secret darshan"? Could it be because I had tried to help an unfortunate girl from New York a few days earlier? Although we are apt to forget it, Baba knows all and sees all, but we certainly can not hope to always understand his ways.

One year at Prasanthi Nilayam, just before the Dasara festival, a girl arrived from New York and I noticed that she seemed to have no luggage whatever and was wearing only a very dirty dress. She didn't have a cent in her pocket and was starving. She was black, and rightly proud of it.

I asked her how she came to be in such a condition and she simply said, "I belong to Swami. He looks after me." It is nonetheless an affront to Swami to come to his ashram in such a dirty state. The poor, love-starved girl was being ignored by everyone. I invited her to my flat so she could wash her dress. Before doing so, she took a comb out of her pocket and a few withered leaves from the decorations used on Baba's chair. They were all her worldly possessions. We had a meal together and then went to the village bazaar to buy her a new kaftan dress and petticoat and a blanket to cover her during the cool nights. I also gave her food coupons so she could obtain meals in the ashram canteen. The poor girl had left a monstrous society in the West, where she felt she was treated like a dog and even starvation seemed a better alternative. She was quite desperate. She eventually returned to the States feeling more confident about the future, after having received strength and help from the Divine. Often life changes to ease and happiness when people spend time here.

This special darshan brought to memory a similar darshan earlier that year, during summer at Kodaikanal. Among the devotees gathered there was a young girl whose *sadhana* (spiritual practice) sometimes took on a rather eccentric expression, such as running after Baba's car when he was driving out of the ashram.

At the time, there was a great deal of service work for devotees to do as they helped clear a building site for extensions to the bhajan hall. Baba directed the work personally, either watching from his balcony or being present in person from time to time. Usually there were more eager hands than needed to do the necessary work.

On the day the work began, as the rising sun sent its first rays over the mountain ridge, this young girl tried in vain to get a place in the line of workers passing baskets loaded with earth and rock one way, from hand to hand, and empty baskets the other. Everybody was in high spirits except the girl. Everywhere she tried to get into the line, she was pushed out. Finally she stood crying in the middle of the building site.

Without thinking I ran to her and pulled her into my place in the line, then sat down on a rock. Suddenly, there was Baba standing right in front of me. There was a radiant light in his eyes, a light of compassion. Those two eyes were shining so brightly I could hardly look into them. It was as if he looked straight into my soul, and soul met soul. The effect was overwhelming and I quickly got up and left.

I took a taxi back to my cottage and instinctively covered my face during the journey. The light of his eyes had penetrated light into the depths of my being. Tears streamed silently down my face. I was deeply moved.

It was a glorious morning. The tall sunflowers in the little garden in front of my cottage nodded their heads cheerfully in the fresh breeze coming in from the mountains. The air was full of the sound of humming bees. All else was still. In the distance I could see a mountain peak with a small white cap of snow. Surrounded by the beauty of nature, I saw everywhere only *Govinda* (one of the many Indian names for the divine), and I was resting in the peace of God's heart.

The Divine
Visits Bombay

In March, 1988, I was fortunate enough to be able to follow
Swami when he visited Bombay. It was a remarkable experience. From the moment he boarded the plane in Bangalore,
just two minutes before its departure, until it landed in Bombay, the flight was charged with high-powered energy. I am
sure the immensely powerful vibrations were felt by everyone
on the aircraft. The crew were very much on their toes, giving the best possible service, and the flight attendant, who
demonstrated the safety equipment while standing right next
to where Baba was seated, was clearly moved.

But even high in the sky there was no rest for the avatar.
The plane had scarcely taken off before a long line of people,
all wishing to do padnamaskar, began to form in the aisle. He
accepted it all for about twenty minutes before retiring to the
first class section to sit quietly. He was the first to leave the
aircraft when it landed in Bombay and was driven away
immediately in a waiting car.

In Bombay, I checked into the Hare Krishna Hotel
located about fifteen minutes' drive from the domestic airport. My two traveling companions were a couple from
Greece. Despite an announcement on the bulletin board that
the hotel was fully booked until April, they accommodated
us.

The hotel, which belongs to the International Society for
Krishna Consciousness, is gracious, functional, and spot-

lessly clean. The flooring throughout is marble and each room has air conditioning, fans, and a separate balcony. All this luxury is made available at a very reasonable cost.

Each morning a few monks sit in meditation in public, giving the place a very peaceful atmosphere. Adjacent to the hotel, separated only by a glass wall, was the Hare Krishna Temple built in ancient Indian architectural style with five richly carved marble domes. The inner courtyard and a two-story building, with beautifully carved balconies supported by graceful columns, were also all in marble. Marble was the only construction material I saw. In the courtyard was a statue of the now deceased founder of the Society, his divine grace A. C. Bhaktivedanta Swami Prabhupada, who was born in Calcutta in 1896. He devoted his life to teaching Vedic knowledge in the English language and was widely respected as a great scholar and teacher. His followers regard him as an enlightened being. The statue depicts the Swami in his usual meditative posture. It had such powerful vibrations that the first time I saw it, I thought it was the real, living Swami himself.

In the evenings, the monks sing bhajans that echo around the walls of the beautiful temple complex. A large orange tree, laden with fruit, occupies the center of the courtyard. On the day of Baba's arrival in Bombay, evening bhajans were held at 6:00 P.M. in the huge Jalan Mandap, a construction of pillars over which a beautifully decorated *shamiana* (patterned canvas) was suspended to give shade from the merciless sun. The mandap is at least twice as big as the Poornachandra Hall at Prasanthi Nilayam, and it was packed. Already on that first day top government officials and many other VIPs had come to pay their respects to Baba.

After greetings had been exchanged, Baba came down the flight of stairs leading from his house, Dharmakshetra. Despite a day packed full of engagements, he looked as fresh as morning dew, smiling sweetly, while a strong wind played in the splendor of his hair. He sat down on his chair on the dais and was greeted silently by the immense crowd who were seeing him again for the first time in two-and-a-half years. At the first glimpse of him, tired and worn faces lit up with joy. Arms were raised above heads, palms together, to express gratitude while some bent their heads to hide freely flowing tears.

After bhajans, I was able to meet the Greek couple I was traveling with in the milling throng in Maha Kali Street. The husband held his light blue sitting cushion high above the heads of the crowd to signal his position. We took an autorickshaw back to our hotel, and thanks to the "cushion banner" always managed to stick together in spite of the immense traffic jams.

The next day was *Ugadi* (Telugu New Year) and at 10:00 A.M. doctoral students from the Sri Sathya Sai Institute of Higher Learning at Prasanthi Nilayam presented a play called "Bhajan Govindam." The drama had been directed by Baba and was only for invited guests. However, by Swami's grace, an invitation was extended to us and we were able to watch the play from fine seats. We were touched by the simplicity and beauty of the play, which had a great impact and lifted everyone spiritually. It may have prompted many to wonder about their own way of life, longing for the harmony and peace that was so graciously and charmingly expressed by the students in the drama.

In the evening, at 5:00 P.M., Baba was to deliver his New Year speech. The mandap was filled to capacity and even the driveway up to his house was packed with people squatting on the road. When the world is burning, who can extinguish that raging fire except the divine?

The former Indian ambassador to Italy gave an inspired opening address. He spoke of ignorance and its devastating side effects—every devil is out today to ruin the world, but to save God's global creation the divine [Sai Baba] has descended to listen to the cry of a harassed humanity, to serve mankind in its hour of greatest need. "He is the guardian of truth in the garden of trust. He is the crusader against injustice. He is the beacon light for all. He who conquers himself is the greatest of all."

Baba then gave his vital New Year message and the vast audience listened with rapt attention. He began his talk by pointing out the depths to which humanity has fallen and emphasized that the way out is through *seva* (selfless service to others). Through service we can conquer egoism and realize the unity that underlies creation. Baba said, "Service (should be) done with the reservoir of love in the heart and done in God-consciousness." He concluded his talk by singing a bhajan. Just as Lord Krishna's voice enchanted the Gopikas, so Baba's voice enchants his devotees. It is a voice that has been heard by millions, from the southern tip of India to the Himalayas.

Somehow after Baba's New Year message I was able to see in a different light the apparent cruelty of life for millions of people in a cosmopolitan city like Bombay. With its eleven million inhabitants, Bombay can be painful to visit. Perhaps all this turmoil is only the birth pains, however severe, of a totally different future for both India and the world — which is being initiated by Baba, who is leading us toward a life of an infinitely higher order.

At each program during the Bombay visit, we were given fine seats with special kindness by the volunteer service workers. At times they even took us by the hand saying, "Come, sit here. You are from Puttaparthi." The volunteers had an extremely busy time but did an efficient job controling the huge crowds and clearing traffic jams. Everything was well-organized and went smoothly. But on no one else was there such pressure as there was on Sathya Sai Baba. Anyone else would have collapsed after five minutes, yet he always looked cool and fresh, beaming with vitality and radiating love and compassion. Nowhere, at any time, was any money sought or collected. On the contrary, everything was free. After

Baba's New Year message the organizers even managed to distribute *prasad* (consecrated food, blessed by God) to each and everyone in the crowd of 50,000 devotees.

The next morning, Bal Vikas programs for children—during which Baba walked graciously among them as they sat happily in front of his Dharmakshetra house—were shown live on TV screens, while people waited in the mandap for bhajans to begin. The Dharmakshetra temple, designed like a lotus flower opening up toward the sky (a symbol for the eternal), is quite a feat of modern architecture. It stands like a monument to purity and beauty, like a promise for a better future and a better humanity.

Baba arrived from the Bal Vikas program a few minutes after 9:00 A.M. and sat on his chair on the dais. That was the signal for bhajans to begin. Many people in the audience had been waiting more than two hours for just this moment. To sing bhajans as one with those thousands of people was a great and moving experience. It illustrated the truth of Baba's statement that, "Unity underlies creation."

We were told that Baba looked after even the smallest detail of all the arrangements. Nothing escaped his ever-watchful eye. Even if he were not personally present, he saw and he knew and he corrected whatever was out of line.

In a talk given by a student before evening bhajans that day, Baba's omnipresence was vividly described. He confirmed that even if Baba were not present, he saw and knew about any wrongdoings and corrected them. It is these students, many of them brilliant, who are the standard-bearers of Baba's message. It is through their example that the overall consciousness of India and its people is being raised.

On Sunday morning Baba gave his last public talk, which again was a great practical and spiritual message for the people of this sprawling city. When, after evening bhajans on that last day, it was announced over the loudspeakers that "This ends the Divine's visit to the city of Bombay," he raised his hands in blessing of the crowd and quietly left the scene in lonely majesty. As his slight figure disappeared, everyone stood in silent homage, instinctively aware that he carried with him the burden of the whole world.

To be greeted the next day by Baba as he boarded the early morning plane leaving Bombay was another memorable experience on a lovely and unforgettable trip. My friends and I were still trying to understand all we had seen and heard, but we were reassured by the thought that one day India will rise like the Phoenix, a symbol of uniqueness, resurrection, and immortality.

Baba's words, as usual, summed things up perfectly, "If you do not feel the call at the sight of human distress and disease, how can you have the determination and dedication to serve the unseen, inscrutable, and mysterious God? When you do not love human beings your heart will have no love for God. Despising brother humans, you cannot at the same time worship God. If you do God will not accept that hypocrisy."

The Mother

In the ancient Aryan culture, which is the culture of the seers, sages, and godmen of all ages who are said to be the salt of this earth, the mother is a sacred person. According to this culture "the mother, father, preceptor should be treated as God and in this the mother occupies the highest position. The mother loves her child, undergoes all sorts of sufferings for its development, will sacrifice anything for its good."

It may be of interest to know that the well-known Western scholar, Max Muller, has said that in the history of the world, the Vedas — written in Sanskrit — and the very foundation of the Aryan culture, fill a gap that no literary work in any other language could fill.

Sri Aurobindo, whose whole philosophy of life was based on this Aryan culture and even went beyond it, says about a society in which the mother, father and guest have very little place and the Divine none at all — the Western commercial society — "in caliber it is debased, in civilization nil and now nearing its height and its fall."

And what does the godman of our time, Sri Sathya Sai Baba, say about a topic which is very dear to him? "Revere the mother as Divine, revere the preceptor (or teacher) as Divine, revere the guest as Divine. Everyone has the Divine in him, the teacher who opened your eyes to the treasures within you, the guest who gave you the splendid chance to render service to the living embodiment of the Divine right in your very home and the mother who gave you life."

The mother occupies a special place in Baba's teachings and he says: "Gratitude for her is absent only among the beasts. . . . Think of all the care, all the love, all the pain and sleeplessness she underwent for your sake and still undergoes for your sake. Be kind, be soft and sweet to her. Do not be rude and raw. Try your best to make her happy, obey her, for she knows much better than you the world and its dangers. . . . If you fail in this you do not deserve this glory of being born as a human being. . . . Today, what do we see when the mother is laid up with high fever, the son runs to a film show. . . . The mother gave you life. You owe your health and happiness to her. She loves you, serves you, she gives you as much as she can and even more. The mother has given us this blood, this body and this individuality and therefore she deserves all consideration and worship. . . . By disregarding the mother we shall never be able to prosper in life and we shall never be able to become good in life."

Similarly the great Swami Vivekananda said, "One doesn't talk about one's mother to others. There is a privacy, a sanctity about one's feelings for one's mother. The name has been called holy once and forever, for what name is there which no lust can ever approach, no carnality ever come near other than the one word mother.

"The mother guards and shapes the child . . . and what is the educational 'method' employed by the mother? Simply her love. It is this love that opens the windows of knowledge and the ways of right thinking, feeling, and action . . . the mother who gave birth to us is creatrix, builder, sustainer, educator, protectress, all in one . . . no wonder, throughout our life, we feel irresistibly drawn toward the mother." As this concept of the mother is rather unknown and almost totally disregarded in the West, it has been included in this book. If lived, many a disaster may be averted.

The Divine Flute Player

In Baba's teachings, we often encounter expressions like "elimination of the mind," and "conquest of the mind." But what do expressions like this really mean? They can be difficult to understand and for the Westerner, almost unintelligible. It is difficult for Westerners to imagine how we might fare in today's world without a mind.

In the Upanishads it is said that our whole mind-consciousness is shot through and through with the threads of desire, and that only by purification of the mind-consciousness can we know and possess our real and eternal self. If we turn from the written word to the spoken word of God, whom we worship in the avatar, we find, Baba tells us, "The mind is a bundle of desires and unless these desires are removed by their roots there is no hope of elimination of the mind, which is a great obstacle on the path of spiritual progress."

If we can eliminate desire, our real soul can then emerge and take the place left vacant by the "desire mind." The elimination of the mind, therefore, does not mean that we become mindless in the sense that we are wandering around like zombies. It means that we substitute our real self, the divinity within us all, for the day-to-day "desire mind" that we mistakenly believe is the real us. We still engage the world around us. That is our duty and obligation, but we see the world for what it really is—a Divine drama—a perfect unfolding of events in which we play our part as we learn lessons and atone for mistakes so that we purify ourselves as we progress toward God and inevitably merge as one.

To get rid of desire, however, amounts to getting rid of ego, and that is a formidable job, a battle, a war with ourselves that can be most easily won by surrender to the divine. Surrender is virtually indispensable. How else can his power work in us? But it must be a surrender of love. An inner fire must be lit into which all is thrown with the divine's name upon it. In that fire all impurities are burned away until a spirit of love arises out of the flame and smoke.

We can have a "preview" of what this "elimination of the mind" is about by withdrawing our mind's sanction of desire. There is nothing new in this; it has always been the principle aim of spiritual discipline. It has been clearly expressed in the Bhagavad Gita as a complete renouncement of desire for the fruits (outcomes or rewards) of actions, a complete annulment of desire itself that brings forward perfect equanimity.

"Elimination of the mind" also means to detach ourselves from thought and opinion. Again, this is difficult to comprehend. Are we supposed to not think? Of course we must think, or we would be reduced to imbeciles. According to the teachings of Indian seers and sages down through the ages, the mind has to convert its normal functioning into something of an infinitely higher order, without ego, bondage, or reaction, and manifesting pure and divine love. Such a mind is no longer a mind in the ordinary sense, but an illuminated, silent, divine mastermind.

Such a silent, intuitive and divine mind is at work here on Earth today, ever watching, guiding, inspiring, encouraging, and guarding us. Sathya Sai Baba says, "I do not think." A strange statement perhaps, at first glance, but his is the direct subtle vision, the supreme reason, "far, far beyond the reach of the mind." He works ceaselessly for our upliftment always. Wherever Baba appears reminds us, with the characteristic and symbolic upward turned movement of his hand, that our main concern in life is to lift our consciousness to a higher level. He pours out over us the divine love that is at the core of all creation, and which in its purity, fragile human nature cannot always bear or even understand.

The goal is self-fulfillment. It may be somewhat far off for most of us, but there are milestones that can indicate whether we are on the right path or not. By *sadhana* (spiritual practice) a stillness can be created in the mind in which there is not a shadow of a wish or a want. This state certainly does not mean inactivity, indeed the greatest works are done in the stillness of the mind. In this stillness the divine's grace can and does descend. A mere look is often enough to establish contact. The soul feels the touch. Deep inside our being something starts vibrating with inexpressible sweetness. Everything, inside and out, is beating in harmony, without words, but full of peace and strength. We become ready to break old ties and replace them with the greater truth of Oneness.

After this sort of experience, ordinary life governed by the senses and centered around a superficial ego seems quite silly, even barren, a lie, a negation of the truth, an imprisonment, a very painful affair. From then on, the soul accepts only ties that are God-ward bound. It listens only to the Divine Flute Player (a reference to Baba, who appeared in earlier times as Lord Krishna and enchanted devotees with his flute playing).

Baba has said, "You need not even read the Gita or the Upanishads. You will hear a Gita especially designed for you if you call upon the Lord in your own heart. He is there installed as your own charioteer. Ask Him and He will answer. Have the form of the Lord before you when you sit quietly in a place for meditation and have His name, that is any Name, on your tongue when you do japam. If you do japam without that picture or form before you, who is to give the answer?" To listen to this present day Gita is the privilege of our time. We must not miss the opportunity.

Baba has told us, "On previous occasions when God has incarnated on earth, the Bliss of recognizing Him in the incarnation was vouchsafed only after the Physical Embodiment had left the world in spite of plenty of patent evidences of His Grace. And the loyalty and devotion they commanded from humanity arose through fear and awe at their superhuman powers and skills or at their imperial and personal authority. But ponder a moment on this Sathya Sai Manifestation in this age of rampant materialism, aggressive disbelief, and irreverence. What is it that brings to it the adoration of millions from all over the world? It is *prema* (selfless love). You will be convinced that the basic reason for this is the fact that this is the supra-worldly Divinity in Human Form."

Puttaparthi, which at the time of Baba's birth was little more than a desert village with no electricity, great scarcity of water, and where few had seen a motor car, is today the Vedic heart of India in all its fullness and splendor, and Baba is the *Veda purusha* (the Divine soul).

PART FOUR

A NEW WAY

OM in the Kremlin

In early March, 1990, a remarkable event took place in Soviet Russia that must surely rate as one of the most astonishing spiritual moments in that country's long history. Over one thousand people packed into St. George Hall in the Kremlin at the end of a week-long conference—a global forum of spiritual leaders and parliamentarians concerned with survival of planet Earth. In attendance were parliament members from the five continents of the world, spiritual leaders of every denomination, world renowned scientists and economists, and famous sociologists and agronomists. Also in attendance were the Secretary-General of the United Nations, the heads of four UN agencies, plus hundreds of observers who had traveled thousands of miles to discuss global survival. The occasion was covered by print and electronic media journalists from all around the world.

While then Soviet chairman, Mikhail Gorbachev, sat at the podium ready to deliver a keynote speech to close the conference, a Hindu Swami, in yellow saffron robes, positioned himself at the speaker's rostrum. He raised his right hand inviting all to listen and follow. The Swami intoned, "Oooommm," and the chamber filled with that ancient sound, the sound of the supreme universal reality.

Mikhail Gorbachev, seemingly completely at ease, chanted "Oooommm." His Foreign Minister, Shevardnadze, after darting a quick look at his boss, chanted "Oooommm."

Everyone began to join in. Three American senators bowed their heads in respect as they recited an unknown holy word. It was the first time in seventy years that a religious or spiritual word had been uttered in the Kremlin, but it seemed neither inappropriate nor extraordinary.

Throughout the conference, there had been an amazing and harmonious exchange of views. For example, Soviet academician Velikhov, a high-powered nuclear physicist, could be seen in earnest conversation with Fritjof Capra, a man concerned with the "values" of physics. Scientists have claimed for centuries that science is value-free; yet here were two men, from opposite ends of the argument, in deep consultation. Similarly, journalists from the East and the West quickly established a rapport, despite vast differences in concepts of free speech and traditions of inquiry and investigation. All seemed to participate actively in the intense group discussions on the need to return to considerate, rather than aggressive, relationships among human beings and between humankind and nature.

The general conclusion appeared to be that most of the ills that threaten us now — war, ecological catastrophe, pervasive poverty, and the strangely malevolent diseases which increasingly prey on us — are due to the fact that we have rejected proper human values. If we fail to embrace these values to determine the way we relate to our fellow human beings in our communities and countries, to our environment and the broader cosmos, then we will pass on to our children not a living planet, but a dead Earth. This, of course, is exactly what the Sathya Sai program — Education In Human Values (EHV) — is all about.

Dr. Artong Jumsai, a member of parliament in Thailand, and a devotee of Sai Baba who has played a central role in the development of EHV in that country, not only attended the international forum but spoke to delegates about the Sathya Sai program.

So successful was Dr. Jumsai's address that he was able to interest Gorbachev in EHV. Gorbachev subsequently announced that all money previously spent on nuclear research, and a portion of the money spent on arms manufacture, would in the future be redirected to improving the environment and would include the introduction of the EHV concept in schools.

From Moscow, Dr. Jumsai traveled to India for a meeting with Baba. When asked if he would give a talk about his experiences at the International Forum concerned with Global Survival, Dr. Jumsai answered, "No more talking—now is the time to act." He did, however, relate what a unique experience it was when the hall in the Kremlin filled with the sacred vibrations of the "Oooommm" chant.

A New Way

India is a country of great contradictions. Enormous untapped natural resources go hand-in-hand with a scarcity of day-to-day commodities. Rich people exploit the poor—treating the poor little better than dogs. Husbands, more often than not, look upon their wives almost as servants, not as partners in life.

One of Baba's most powerful weapons against people's overwhelming greed, the wish to always want more, is his program called "Ceiling on desires." Devotees pledge themselves to forego the endless acquisition of material goods and undertake a personal plan to phase out unnecessary luxuries and self-indulgence and eliminate waste and extravagance. It has had a great impact in India and has now spread to many other countries. In one of the most affluent European countries it has been introduced under the title *Die neue Becheidenheit* (The New Modesty).

In the West, all the values of this century have been undermined and are now fast collapsing. Society itself is breaking up. Everywhere today, whether it be in the East or West, there seems to be great uncertainty, even chaos arising from people's greed. In the midst of this turmoil, however, the foundation for a new way, the Sathya Sai Education in Human Values (EHV), has been made available by Sai Baba.

In every respect EHV requires a reversal of present day values, particularly for the education of the young, although it applies just as much to adults who aspire to live a higher and better life. We adults must re-educate ourselves. The ordinary nature of humanity is egoistic, vulgar, and mainly interested in seeking physical and materialistic pleasure. These thoughts and attitudes have to be overcome and reshaped for they are out of touch with the new way. By comparison they are ugly, dark, and deluded. According to Baba humanity is suffering from the "disease" of wrong thoughts, attitudes, and lifestyles. But the new way leads to a life of light and balance, beauty and joy, so it is the very opposite of the present state of affairs. It is a profound and far-reaching way of teaching.

First of all the new way involves a rejection of the present method of teaching. It revolutionizes the whole aim of education today, which according to Sri Aurobindo is the most ingeniously complete machine for murder that human stupidity ever invented, and murder not only of the body but of the soul. Our so-called modern education methods are false, empty, and mechanical. Students go through a rigid and cast-iron course of acquiring knowledge, which gives them real knowledge of nothing. It is education that has no soul, hence the growing sense of frustration everywhere in the minds of the younger generation.

Sai Baba has said, "The educational system is the bank on which the nation draws a check whenever it wants strong, reliable, skilled workers. If it goes bankrupt, as it has very nearly gone today, it is a national disaster."

The new educational way does not mean stuffing a student's memory with information that is of little use other than being re-cycled for tests and examinations. Instead, it seeks to develop the personality, the true self. It is a higher education that above all aims at raising the student's consciousness, to bring out the best there is in them and provide an understanding of the true nature of human life. As an end result of their academic training, they can face the world with strength and confidence, and know the joy of living, working, earning, and caring, and providing for others. It is about life, of life, and for life. Its intention is to develop all the students' faculties.

The Sathya Sai EHV program means a radical change in the student's whole attitude to life. The students of the Sri Sathya Sai Institutes for Higher Learning are living examples of the profound effect this type of study can have on the mind. Before long their faces say it all; they reflect an awareness of the spiritual reality of life, and are full of life and joy.

Dr. Artong Jumsai has helped give the EHV program a shape that is eminently suitable for Western countries. He has spoken about the program all over the world and at the United Nations.

As a scientist, Dr. Jumsai worked for two years in the American space research program in California where he concentrated on the Viking project to land a spacecraft on the surface of Mars. His specific task was to design an electronic system to control the actual moment of landing, a crucial element of the mission.

Dr. Jumsai tells of spending countless hours, and many sleepless nights, trying to solve the vast problems involved. Try as he might, a solution eluded him. Finally Dr. Jumsai traveled to some nearby mountains to meditate on the problem in seclusion. During a period of meditation, the entire idea of a landing system came to him in a moment. He returned to his work place, tested the idea, and found it worked perfectly. Today, Dr. Jumsai often relates the story to illustrate how intuition starts working when the mind is still.

Eventually Dr. Jumsai journeyed to Puttaparthi with two other well-known scientists, and the group was granted an interview with Sai Baba. The three scientists, the only people in the room with Swami, were flabbergasted to discover that he knew far more about science than they did. Swami apparently revealed to them secrets of science that they had never heard before. According to Dr. Jumsai, "He was a much greater scientist than we were."

Dr. Jumsai later returned to Puttaparthi to attend an international Bal Vikas (Sai Spiritual Education for the children of devotees) conference and recalls how Swami, at the time, invited him to become involved in EHV. "If you do that," Baba said, "I will look after you and your business." Dr. Jumsai accepted the invitation.

At the time, Dr. Jumsai had a factory in Bangkok and employed a watchman to guard the premises at night. The watchman, however, was lazy, and each night would retire to the guardhouse, lock the door, and go to sleep. One night he received the shock of his life when, after he had locked the door, a man suddenly appeared in his room and physically grabbed and shook him, saying, "Do your duty well." He then disappeared as quickly as he had appeared. The sudden appearances of the mystery visitor went on for three nights, until the watchman was at a breaking point. On the morning of the fourth day, he rushed frantically into the office of Dr. Jumsai, only to be confronted by a picture of Swami hanging on the wall. "It's him, with all that hair," shouted the watchman, pointing to the picture of Swami, as he tried to explain his nightly ordeal to Dr. Jumsai. Needless to say, from that time on the watchman performed his duty extremely well! It was a graphic demonstration that Baba was keeping his promise to look after Dr. Jumsai.

Later, Baba was to give Dr. Jumsai a strong test. In fact, he was to have a narrow escape from bankruptcy and in his despair cried out, "Is this the way Baba looks after me!" In an interview some time after, Baba said, "You lost everything, I know it all, but I wanted to test you."

Indeed, it seems that Baba had extended his protection to Artong Jumsai many years previously. Dr. Jumsai tells this story; "I was born in Bangkok over fifty years ago, during the Second World War. The Japanese came to Thailand and took over the country and there was a lot of bombing. I was too young to remember, but I recall my mother telling me that one day a Buddhist monk came to our house and offered her a small package. My mother said it contained something sacred. The monk told her to put what appeared to be a powder under the roof, and we would be saved. Then he disappeared. My mother did as he asked and spread the powder under our roof. The result was amazing. After many bombing attacks all the houses around us were blown to pieces. Ours was the only house left standing and we were saved. Everything else in the area was flattened."

During an international conference on EHV in Hamburg in May, 1989, Dr. Jumsai related a story that showed the extent of the behavioral change that can be achieved by the program. As the EHV program in Bangkok became busier, and the number of people interested "grew and grew," the time came to move into bigger premises. A new place was found in a different area of town. As is the custom in Thailand, people arriving for the meeting removed their footwear at the door. Unfortunately, when it was time to leave, they found all their shoes had vanished! The most likely culprits seemed to be the many slum children in that part of town. But as these children became interested in what was being taught, and started attending classes in the new center, the shoes gradually began to reappear!

As time passed, and they received a flow of love from the teachers they met at the school, many of these former slum children changed completely into lovely, charming youngsters. At Prasanthi Nilayam, a student once told Dr. Jumsai, "Before we came to Swami we were street dogs, today we are street lamps." Those associated with the EHV program in Bangkok confidently expect that within two years it will help bring down the crime rate, street accidents, and drug addiction.

Later on, Dr. Jumsai became Minister for Education. His influence and initiative have led to the passing of legislation that will ensure that EHV is integrated into Thailand's education system over a three-year period. There is no doubt that EHV plays an all important and fundamental role in Baba's teaching.

The Flowerbeds

During a talk at Prasanti Nilayam, Dr. Jumsai told of a simple experiment carried out by an EHV class. Seeds of marigold were sown in two separate boxes, with similar soil, and watered equally every day. The plants in one of the boxes were given a lot of attention and care, while those in the other box received none. The plants receiving all the care grew into tall, straight marigolds with big, beautiful blossoms, while the others grew stunted and had small, insignificant heads. The astonishing difference has been repeated in similar, although much more intense experiments, carried out by the famous botantist, Dr. Bhose, in Calcutta. He has written a number of books about the subject.

It is fair, I think, to conclude that students who are taught under ordinary educational systems around the world can be likened to the flowers with small blossoms. They are prepared for a dreary, mediocre, and meaningless existence and find neither joy nor beauty in life. A certain amount of knowledge is imparted to them that they are expected to store and remember. Fear of forgetting what they have been taught and getting poor marks often means that they stop thinking for themselves. At this point teaching ends. It is hardly surprising, therefore, that few students have any respect for their teachers, who seem little more than robots or computers on legs. It is a problem that affect students all around the world.

But education is far more than just the accumulation of knowledge. Surely a teacher has a greater responsibility to himself or herself, to students, their parents, and indeed to the world. It is teachers who help form the new generation. According to Baba, the teacher is the most important person in society. But are our teachers aware of this responsibility?

The true teacher is a guide and friend who teaches by example. Such teachers create an atmosphere of mutual sympathy and confidence between themselves and their students. The teachers' first responsibility is to teach the primary values of life — truth, right conduct, love, peace, and non-violence — as a basis for later academic learning. It implies that they must look within themselves and see their own faults and limitations. They must clearly be aware of the dangers of negative thinking and its ability to drag down not only their own minds, but those of their students. Teachers must be enlightened enough to recognize the importance of the human values laid down by Sathya Sai Baba and incorporate them into the techniques they use and the subject matter they teach.

I am sure it will soon become obvious to teachers, as indeed it already is to many, that present methods are failing. They will realize the urgent need for a new and creative teaching methodology that leads to an expansion of consciousness, within which there is the opportunity to develop greater sensitivity.

Teachers can use the subject matter they teach as a means to open the minds of students. For example, in mathematics it can be pointed out that mathematics is order, the universe is order, and intelligence is order. This can be contrasted with the disorderly way that most students live their lives, both internally and externally. In time, this will bring about a change in the students minds, as they listen to and follow the teachers appeal for, and example of, order. Academic learning is vital, of course, but so is learning about how to meet life in a sane and balanced way.

EHV is a form of teaching that is not based on comparison, the life-style of many people these days — "He has a better car than I have," or "They have a bigger house than us" — with all its jealousy, conflict, and antagonism. Students learn simply to observe, without always having to pass judgment about whether it is good or bad. They learn what beauty is, not only outer beauty but the beauty within themselves, a beauty that only exists where there is great love and compassion. Without the strength of the beauty, we can never come upon the truth of life. Surely it is this, with which a true teacher is most concerned.

The Sathya Sai Educational System is, therefore, aimed at nothing less than revolutionizing existing educational programs. Many young people have begun to discard such traditional educational programs as they relate neither to the students nor the world around them.

Students educated within the framework of EHV can be likened to the beautiful marigolds grown in the flower beds that received intensive care and attention. The students grow straight, full of vitality and intelligence, and spread joy and well-being around them. Their life adopts a totally different rhythm. The reason, I believe, is that EHV is orientated toward a higher dimension of consciousness, to the *atma* (the spark of God within, the soul, the innermost reality) and this creates a radical change in the student's thinking.

There have, in the course of time, been many different programs, religious, philosophical, and idealistic that aimed at changing the human mind. All have failed. The human mind is as brutal as ever. To me, the true answer to the dreadful dilemma the world is in lies in intelligence and love as formulated by Sathya Sai Baba in his potent EHV program. It is of the greatest importance that his name goes with it, for the name Sathya Sai is accompanied by all the dynamic love and unlimited possibilities for which it stands. Without the name, it is rather a tame affair.

The Sathya Sai educational program includes all the universal human values but *dharma* (right action) is the basis on which all the other values rest—a fundamental to the new civilization and better world for which it aims. We live in a world where few trust each other, where all religions, civilizations, and cultures have failed to bring about peace. Into such a world the divine has descended. His leelas, performed by the thousands and which defy all laws of modern physics, serve only one purpose—to make people aware of his divinity. People who have had a concrete experience of them ask themselves, "Who is this mysterious figure who can do things that nobody else in the world can do?" They are then drawn closer to his teachings. This is the physical aspect of Baba's leelas and their intention.

When people experience the great calm and peace this godhead, often by a mere glance, can instill in them—they change psychologically to a state of being in which it is impossible for them intentionally to cause harm to another human being. This is the broad concept of nonviolence, which as Dr. Jumsai pointed out in his talk, includes all the other values.

> Who is he who moves so silently among
> us with such wonderful poise,
> Such unutterable love and compassion,
> With a strange power to read the innermost
> secrets of our hearts
> And who makes us all live his message of
> Love.
> He is none other than Sai.

The
Human Mind
is in Great Danger

During a visit to New York in mid-May 1990 I was over-whelmed by the contradictions and stresses evident in the people's lifestyles and attitudes, and the contrast in condi-tions and surroundings between the various neighborhoods of this massive metropolis. Some aspects of life in New York must surely be among the most efficient and affluent in the world. For example, one of the best libraries in the world—a huge, magnificent building guarded by two lions—is in New York. The latest information in science, art, literature, com-merce, and any other discipline can be obtained simply by using the keyboard on one of the many computers installed there. Sometimes the sheer availability of information can be overpowering—such as the time I attempted to locate a suit-able book publisher and was presented with a list of four thousand companies! Eventually it was Baba, not computers, who came to my rescue in the matter, guiding me through a strange set of circumstances and coincidences to the right place.

There are also some fine museums in New York. But instead of visiting those museums, I chose, on a lovely spring day in May, to sit in Central Park under a cherry tree in full bloom and feel its life energy, its pulse, its beauty and be immensely refreshed. For what is art but an opening of the sealed doors of the soul; in silent communication with nature the doors open and we can feel the presence.

Afterward I visited the Metropolitan Museum of Art and I saw some fine works of art from Eastern civilizations, and Dutch, Flemish, French, and Russian art of extraordinary strength and beauty. I was astonished to find that art from the United States was not represented at all!

In America it is the entertainment industry that floods the minds of the people, and above all television. In private homes, TV sets are installed everywhere, in living rooms, bedrooms, and even the stretch limousines have TV sets. Night after night, year in year out, like true addicts, people watch vulgar films about crime, murder, and sex. It is difficult to believe that constant exposure to this sort of material does not have a detrimental and coarsening influence on human thought and action. It is no longer the "ultimate weapon" that is threatening us but the development of the mind, which, dulled by this endlessly purveyed, insidious rubbish has become a similar menace to human welfare. The human mind is in great danger.

Baba has warned us of another factor that makes the mind insensitive and brutal. In a discourse to students Swami said, "People today are behaving in a manner worse than that of wild animals in the forest. They have become cruel, pitiless and hard-hearted. There is no sympathy or understanding between people. The main reason for this condition is the kind of food that is consumed. Be careful about the food you eat. See that it is conducive to your health and happiness."

Baba's use of terms like "cruel, pitiless and hard-hearted" have special relevance to much of the behavior in New York. The one characteristic feature of this biggest city in the world is that it is in the grip of an immense fear. Like a gigantic spectre, fear overshadows the entire metropolis and seems to penetrate the whole atmosphere; fear has become part of daily life.

It is not unusual for people to put three or four locks on the entrance door to their houses or flats, which is securely bolted from the inside. In many areas, shops keep their doors locked throughout the day and to gain entry to make a purchase you must first ring an external bell. Never before has the crime rate been so high in New York as it is today. I stayed in an apartment building for just a few days and in that time my neighbor was robbed as she tried to enter her flat.

These conditions are the price — and it is a terrible one — that is paid by a society that is ruled by capitalism. There are big pockets of abject poverty, appalling housing conditions, and people are alienated from each other and their surroundings. There is no real love or affection. And in the absence of real love, a life centered around lust and indulgence of the senses has assumed great importance. Similarly, because there is no richness of inner life, external entertainment has assumed vast significance. Because there is no beauty of living, of feeling, or thinking, no real beauty even of the body, all manner of devices and techniques to create false beauty exist.

Yet underneath it all, there is a feeling that things are in a state of fermentation. More and more people are seeking a way out of an aimless and very painful existence. They are determined to find the purpose and truth of life and seem aware that it can only be found by seeking in earnest, and not by people seeking amusement or expressing hatred and other kindred feelings. Even people who don't seem to want anything other than the squalor that surrounds them feel a certain emptiness in their lives. The greatest problem, however, for those who want to live a life of a higher order, is the difficulty in resisting the overwhelming pressure from the negative forces that surround them and drag them down. In America today, people trying to pursue a spiritual life must be very strong.

The meaning of creation is for humanity to find its true self. The secret of the avatar is that he transforms humankind into the image of his own inner being. He seeks to help us to understand the confusion and the sorrow in our hearts. He makes us look into ourselves and ask, "Why have I become so narrow-minded, so small hearted, so completely wrapped up in myself, so childish in my desires?" And as we ask ourselves these questions, we begin to become aware of our own dullness. In the very agony of this realization, we change. That is all Baba wants from us; a radical change of our whole being and method of thinking. To achieve this, we need self-discipline and order in our lives.

We should come to this godhead not for the sake of his leelas—though they are on a scale that is without precedence in human history, as is his own manifestation—but for the guidance he unfailingly offers us. In a world where people do not believe in anything they cannot see, hear, touch, taste, or smell, a manifestation of his power is necessary to convince us of his divinity, and the urgent need to put his words into practice.

Sai Baba was born in 1926 and since then has continued to confound scientists, upset the known laws of physics, and stun all those who witness his prodigious acts. Witnesses tell of raising the dead, cancer victims in the last stages cured unexpectedly, quadraplegics and paraplegics who regain the use of their legs without difficulty, and of the blind who after his intervention find their sight restored. Also well-documented is his ability to multiply food, his powers to calm the fury of nature, and the materialization of a massive array of precious and semi-precious objects. He does not want money or even compensation. The message he launches to the world is the fundamental one of all religions. He is able to demonstrate that his prodigious acts are beyond the perception of our sensory organs and, therefore, another reality exists.

People who have been to India bring back this testimony, "He is a master who clears up your doubts. He tells you what is right and what is wrong, and what you need to do to reach the door of the unknown."

In 1990, Don Mario Mazzoleni along with a physician, Dr. Giancarlo Rosati, and others participated in a conference at the Department of International Studies given by the faculty of Political Science at Padua University in Italy. It was called simply, "The Sai Baba Case." Don Mario, a priest and theology teacher in Rome, has said, "I saw him with my own eyes cure four persons of cancer already in metastasis, bald from their chemotherapy treatments. They returned home perfectly normal after Sai Baba's intervention. One day it was pouring rain at Puttaparthi. Sai Baba came out to meet his devotees. Above our heads appeared a kind of clearing, from which the sun appeared. In the rest of the ashram it was raining heavily, but we saw the sun."

His very presence creates a stir in the hearts of those who come to see him. There is such wonderful poise, such unutterable love and compassion, such simplicity of Truth and wisdom in everything he does and says that invariably the doors of our closed hearts are opened. If we come with empty hands, so to speak, and because we are in earnest quest for the Truth, we will meet him. A mere glance from him can transport us to another dimension of consciousness in which we get a foretaste of the oneness of mankind, that all is Brahman (God), and that realization is the way to a creative freedom.

The very foundation of Baba's teaching is that "all is Brahman (God)." We have to become aware of it and he shows us how to do that. It is a spiritual change of consciousness that alone can make life worth living and rescue it from its present distressed and meaningless state.

On my last day in New York, before I returned to the countryside, Baba blessed me with a visit, a clear and loving darshan. His face appeared clearly before me, his eyes looked softly at me as I was preparing to leave.

It is said in the Swetaswatara Upanishad that to be one with the inner core of all life (Brahman) is the purpose and truth of all creation, and it puts us in tune with "the delight of existence."

> Thou (Brahman) art man and woman,
>   boy and girl;
> old and worn thou walkest bent over a staff;
> thou art the blue bird and the green
> and the scarlet-eyed. . . .[1]

---

[1]Swetaswatara Upanishad, IV, 3, Y.

The
Himalayan Climb

Even if we had a hundred years to reach the higher self, it would not be possible without a teacher who shows us the way. We need a teacher who will let us aspirants move forward at our own pace and find God in our own way, through any religion or no religion. We need a teacher who opens our soul to God, as the flower opens for the sun, which is God, but such a teacher is very rare. Today, however, just such a rare teacher, Baba, is showing thousands of people how to find their lost, but true, identity.

The job is not easy. It can be likened to an ascent of Mount Everest, where Mount Everest is synonymous with the higher self. Only the guide (Baba) knows the way, which at the lower levels passes through the equivalent of a dense jungle. The guide can show the pitfalls to those who want to leave the oppressive atmosphere below to scale the heights. He can show us how to clear a passage when the path is overgrown with thorny bushes and how to use an axe to cut down dense foliage through which the sun cannot shine. The guide tells us mountaineers when to put on spiked boots so as to not lose a foothold on the steep terrain. He warns us to be constantly aware throughout the climb, for the way is difficult and few make it to the top.

In fact the guide tells us he can count on the fingers of one hand those who, up until now, have achieved the climb. Once there the mountaineer is above it all, having left the lower nature behind. Our whole being is penetrated by the pure and wonderfully healing mountain air. We are in the region of the highest *Prasanthi* (undisturbed inner peace) that sends its soothing rays of peace down over a suffering humankind. But it is not all who want to reach the top, nor is it necessary. It is enough to become good mountaineers, says the Guide.

Whatever the case, the ascent remains difficult. It is our lower nature with its falsehood, hypocrisy, and negative feelings — fear, bitterness, prejudice, and jealousy — that have to be cleared out of the way. These are the thorny bushes that block the path on the upward journey. Some of these traits become so ingrained that they have to be cut out at the roots, or they sprout again like weeds. A good example is jealousy and its faithful companion, criticism of others, which has become almost like a popular disease. We have to be alert to the constant effort required to uproot just this one bad quality.

Criticism of others is mean under all circumstances and meanness will quickly make us lose our footing on the mountain path of spiritual life. It is a fact that negative, or anti-divine feelings can even ruin our health. We have to protect ourselves by taking the necessary precautions, just as we would take preventative measures at the onset of a plague. Criticism of others is just such a plague, and the measure to be taken against it is to clear out all the adverse thinking, not only from the conscious mind, but the subconscious. If the roots are left in, the weed will come up again.

Often we will meet with the most obstinate resistance from our own minds. Perhaps we have taken a firm resolve not to be angry anymore, but before we realize it, anger overwhelms us like lightning. We have lost the control we were seeking to impose. The best answer is to be ever vigilant. Where the inner terrain is steepest, it can be necessary to put on our spiked boots, puncture the ego, and refuse to put up with any more of its whims.

We have to educate the ego. If it misbehaves, it cannot just be allowed to have its own way. Unfortunately many parents make this mistake today in the name of "freedom" when bringing up their children. But it is a misunderstood freedom. Later in life the child suffers, for it has not been shown the right path, and the parents suffer, too, because their children have chosen a wrong track in life and get lost.

The mind is the strongest thing there is in the body, and like Mount Everest, difficult to conquer. As recorded in the Bhagavad Gita, Arjuna says to Lord Krishna, "Even an elephant cannot drag as the mind does, it is the nursery of waywardness, its obstinacy is also very powerful, it is a terrible screw." But Krishna puts his mind to rest and assures him, "The mind can be mastered through practice and detachment." So we have to be on our guard against becoming attached to feelings that drag the mind down into the subconscious, we must learn not to identify with them. Again, it is not easy. Indeed it is something we all tend to do. But Krishna's immortal words to Arjuna on the eve of the famous Kurukshetra war come to our rescue.[2] "Get up," said Krishna, "and get ready for the battle, you are sure to win." And of course there is a battle to get rid of all the impurities in the mind — anger, fear, doubt, malice, greed, envy, vindictiveness — to become ready to receive the higher forces of peace, light, and bliss.

Baba has said, "The realization of the reality, through spiritual discipline, is an arduous enterprise as fraught with calamity as playing with fire or fighting with tigers or battling with barbarian hordes. One has to be alert, vigilant, and fully trained to meet all emergencies." To me, this is a symbolic reference by Baba that illustrates the difficult and sometimes dangerous thoughts we must contend with as they emerge from the murky depths of our subconscious mind. His color-

---

[2]Recorded in the Bhagavad Gita, the war is an historical event that symbolizes the struggle between the opposing forces of good and evil.

ful words compare the nature and extent of the struggle to situations that can literally mean life or death and reflect the fierce determination we must summon up if we are to win the battle for spiritual life.

Baba continues his description, "Man is the monarch of all animals; we are the most glorious chance among all living beings. Though the elephant lives longer, the lion is more fierce, the eagle more far seeing, the cock more punctual in early rising, the cow more imbued with the spirit of sacrifice, we have in us vast potentialities that can be brought out by proper culture.

"If only we intensify our thirst for God, we can live in perpetual content, instead of groveling in perpetual discontent, pining for land, buildings, bank balance, furniture, status, power, authority, and all such trivial satisfactions. At last, when human beings are about to leave the world, as leave we must, we are confronted by a more urgent, a more personal problem, 'What is to happen to me?' — and we have no more time to discover the answer or to prepare for something good to happen. In fact, if we tried we could have known the reality and gone with a smile, instead of a groan or a whine. Human beings are born with a helpless, lamenting cry; they should die with the smile of happy joy. That is the purpose of the years between.

"All good things have to be done the hard way. Ease and elevation cannot go together. Hardships keep one always alert and in trim. They reveal hidden resources of skill and intelligence, they toughen fortitude and deepen the roots of faith.

"Wealth is worshiped as God; pride has become a creed; selfishness is entrenched in the intellect. The ego is flaunted and desires have become an adornment. Righteousness has become a mere figurehead in the world. Compassion has dried up; gentility has waned; hypocrisy has become the hallmark of life; love and affection have become lustful afflictions. The scriptures are disregarded. Life has become a burden and the mind has gone astray. Gratitude as a virtue has evaporated. In the Kali age these have become the qualifications of educated persons. Alas! What shall I say about the plight of humanity when humanness has fallen so low?"

Is there then no hope? Are we totally unfit to live a higher, spiritual life? It cannot be. The very goal of life is to realize the reality, what is needed is that we change. As Baba has said, "The most important thing is a change of consciousness." And further, "You need not all become *Madhava* (God), it is enough if you become *manava* (human)."

We can conclude from Baba's words that at present we are not acting in a very human way. How, then, do we set about the task? The way is to change our mental attitude so that each time a negative feeling rises to the surface of our minds, we replace it with an opposite, positive feeling. For example, hatred with kindness, envy with understanding, anger with calm, fear with self-confidence, and above all, not to meet others with a suspicious attitude.

Then slowly or quickly—according to the amount of effort we are prepared to expend—we will change. We will begin to meet our fellow creatures with an open mind and a smile. More often than not, we will be treated accordingly—because one attracts the other. Positive thinking has a considerable, elevating affect for when we exercise self-discipline or *sadhana* (spiritual discipline), we provide the opportunity for our higher nature to begin working within us.

Instead of being dragged down into the darkness of the subconscious, our mind lifts up toward the inner light in each of us, the embodiment of the higher self. As we progress along the spiritual path, we can actually come to see and experience this light. It has a wonderful healing effect and can cure any disease of the mind or body. In this state of mind, it is impossible to think in a negative way. It has been said that Baba is "the light of the soul." But constant effort and awareness is needed. Indeed, why should it be otherwise? There would be no sense of achievement, all would reach the summit without any personal effort, no lessons would be learned. Without lessons, effort, and achievement there would be no change, the world would remain as it is. So instead we make our arduous mountain climb and discover many beautiful stages to pass through on the way up, that the air is much purer and more refreshing, and that the journey itself is fascinating.

Deep down in our being is our true self that, in essence, is at one with our higher self, God, the Reality, the Higher Consciousness, or whatever other name we choose to give it. We suffer because our true self has been covered by a facade. We have cultivated it ourselves, we were not born with it, and it is only ourselves that can remove it. In one of his Dasara talks Baba said, "The human nature is false." J. Krishnamurti expressed it slightly differently when he once said, "You are all wearing a mask." According to Krishnamurti when two or more people talk together, the masks involved entertain each other, like actors in a theater. As most people know, appearances can be deceptive, but in spiritual life it is the true being under that appearance that must be uncovered. When this happens, we are on our way toward the higher self and will come to know all the blessedness that contact with it brings.

Love, then, which is at the center of ourselves and at the center of Sai Baba's teachings, will find its true place in our hearts. It can heal any situation, it is a force that dissolves all hostility and misunderstanding and illness. It harmonizes the mind so that where there was once opposition and fear, cooperation and trust will prevail. We find, sometimes to our surprise, that this force of love and harmony is released from within ourselves.

I am convinced that it is from India that the impulse for a new and better world goes out. It is worth noting what Sri Aurobindo had to say on the subject in his book, *The Human Cycle*: "The renascence of India is as inevitable as the rising of tomorrow's sun, and the renascence of a great nation of three hundred million with so peculiar a temperament, such unique traditions and ideas of life, so powerful an intelligence and so great a mass of potential energies cannot but be one of the most formidable phenomena of the modern world."[3]

Sri Aurobindo goes on to say that it is only the avatar who can lead humankind onward "for the secret of his force is spiritual" and it is done alone by the majestic stream of love that flows from him.

When he (Baba) is the guide the difficult labor of the journey is considerably eased. He remolds our whole being with his divine hand, although that remolding is not always a painless affair! He makes us acutely aware of how dangerous it is to think in a negative or anti-divine way. He clears the passage for those who open themselves to his help for the higher forces to do their work in us. His touch brings the utmost calm and joy to the soul. He is the living sun of light.

Some may think they can go on as they are, but they are merely hiding their heads in the sand like an ostrich. In a spiritual sense, and more and more in an everyday sense, "the world is burning." The possibility of change is here and now. It is now that we must act to clear from our minds habitual negative attitudes (fear, hatred, distrust, jealousy, suspicion, pride, anger, greed, lust) that prevail everywhere and cause the sad plight of our world.

The power of thought is enormous and if we practice thinking right thoughts, if we impose our will on our minds and insist that it steadfastly replaces wrong thoughts with these right thoughts, we begin to feel the Divine presence in ourselves. Then everything changes, life becomes full. When the doorway between the higher and lower aspects of ourselves is open, when the connecting passage has been cleared, contact can be established so that the union of the soul (the individual) with the Soul (Divine) can take place. It is this

---

[3]Sri Aurobindo, *Human Cycle, Ideal of Human Unity, War and Self-Determination* (Pondicherry, India: Sri Aurobindo Ashram Trust, 1985), p. 314.

release that all, consciously or unconsciously, are seeking. That union is our *Sanathana Dharma* (eternal path). The Vedas tell us that God is the inner Reality of all beings, all is enveloped by God, all this is God. A manifestation of this Divine principle is here, living on earth at this moment. It is all that actually matters. We live in "the hour of God."

It is particularly on festival days at the Prasanthi Nilayam ashram, when he silently and gently walks among his students (now over two thousand at various campuses) who on these special days gather as his feet to show their love for him, that we can experience Baba in all his divinity. Clearly this younger generation, starting out in a new way and educated in accordance with EHV principles, will have a quite different, confident approach to life compared to most other young people. They have learned the art of thinking positively; they have been taught life's reality and learned that it has a purpose. Their calm, confident behavior speaks for itself and is in sharp contrast to the disillusionment and weariness affecting most modern youth—who feel a great need to know just where they are going.

Baba has created a new way of education that teaches the art of living and of self-fulfillment, and thus reaches into the spiritual sphere. He has opened a new dimension in life of co-operation, peace, knowledge, and beauty that lays the foundations for a better and happier world.

Oh God, thou who art one with all creation,
With the innermost self of everyone,
Thou who so often has filled me with thy blessed
    presence,
let all know, O Lord, that thou art here on earth at
    this moment
and have come to return man to his inherent soul-
    nature of joy.

A Reading from the *Book of Bhrigu*

In the first week of May, 1990, while on my way to New York, I made a two-day stopover in Bombay to try and get a reading from the famous *Book of Bhrigu*. Phyllis Krystal, in her brilliant book about her experiences with Baba, called *Sai Baba: The Ultimate Experience*, explains that she first heard of the *Book of Bhrigu* from a friend. She and her husband discovered "that there were several copies of the original text in the care of pandits who were able to translate it from the original language in which it was written. . . . We had been told that this extraordinary book is mentioned in the Bhagavad-Gita and had originally been written on palm leaves by a sage called Bhrigu who is reported to have received the contents during deep meditation. It describes the lives of certain people who would arrive at some future time to consult it."[4]

Phyllis eventually found a pandit in Bombay who had custody of a copy of the book, written on palm leaves, and I obtained his address from her.

I stayed overnight at the same hotel I had used two years earlier when Baba was visiting Bombay. The next morning, as I was trying to make arrangements at the reception to hire a taxi for the one-and-a-half-hour drive to the pandit's home, a gentleman who had apparently overheard my conversation

[4]Phyllis Krystal, *Sai Baba: The Ultimate Experience* (Dorset, UK: Element Books, 1990), pp. 20, 21.

came forward. He said he was going in that direction and invited me to join him. Two other men were in the rear seat of the car and we soon discovered that we all came from the State of Andhra Pradesh (Sai Baba's birthplace). They were delighted to learn I was a devotee of Baba's. After a pleasant drive through the sprawling city of Bombay, which took an hour-and-a-half, I was dropped off within walking distance of my destination.

The pandit lived on the first floor of a large apartment house in a nice area of Bombay near the sea. I rang the doorbell, and almost immediately it was opened by the pandit himself, as though he had been expecting me. Everything had gone so smoothly I began to get the funny feeling that perhaps this whole episode had been prearranged! I was asked inside and introduced myself to the learned man, telling him only that I was on my way to New York to see my son and daughter-in-law.

I had prepared a list of the most important events in my life in case he wanted to know them, but he didn't ask any questions, other than my date of birth, so I volunteered nothing. He then asked me to go downstairs with him to the courtyard. He indicated I should take off my hat and shoes and step out into the sunlight. I did so, but had to leap quickly back into the shade as the asphalt was burning hot. In the end he allowed me to wear my flat Indian sandals. The pandit then took out a ruler, not the normal kind marked in centimeters or inches, but something that looked like a scientific or astrological ruler. "I am going to measure your shadow," he said.

When he finished, we returned to his apartment where he sat down at his desk, took out pen and paper, and began writing some strange looking calculations. He told me he was making calculations based on the measurement of my shadow. Then, from what appeared to be an endless number of palm leaves, he took out one bundle of leaves. From that bundle he selected just one leaf. He showed it to me saying,

"It is written in Sanskrit." The text was executed in exquisite handwriting, almost like a work of art in itself. It looked as though each letter had been formed with infinite care, perfection, and love.

He handed me a writing pad and pen so I could take down his reading. He began: "You have a long life . . . your guru is Sathya Sai Baba" (I had not mentioned I had a guru of any sort). "You do the Gayatri Mantra. . . ." (I was astonished at this. I chant the mantra morning and night, every day, regardless of where I am.) You are a high incarnation."

The pandit continued, saying, among other things, "Baba loves you . . . you are now writing a book about Baba" (indeed, I was and this volume is it!). "The book will be successful . . . you are very happy in India . . . in this body your mission is yoga meditation, writing books, staying with Baba, Gayatri Mantra and social work." I then asked what was meant by social work. He replied, "Writing books. Baba will help you."

The pandit then went on to make a number of completely accurate statements about my son and daughter-in-law concerning their work, personalities, health, and relationship with each other and with me. I was particularly surprised when he announced that my daughter-in-law had just recently been awarded a Guggenheim grant for her work as an artist. He concluded with a number of statements of a highly personal nature relating to my own life.

I left the pandit feeling completely confused. I struggled to grasp the fact that thousands of years ago this most beautifully handwritten leaf, from a historically famous text, had been compiled about me, my son, and my daughter-in-law! Yet the facts read by the pandit were accurate and beyond dispute, despite the fact that he had never seen or heard of us, and was given no information whatsoever about us. To this day he has not even set eyes on my son and daughter-in-law. Time alone will test some of the predictions contained in the

Book of Bhrigu about how the future will effect the three of us. Clearly there is much that is beyond the ability of the human mind to fathom.

Celebration of Joy

Preparations were made several months beforehand for the celebration of Sri Sathya Sai Baba's 65th birthday on November 23, 1990. A museum was built and opened for Baba's birthday. It has three grand domes representing the three Sai Avatars—the former Shirdi Sai who died eight years before the present Parthi Sai was born, and the one to come, Prema Sai. Prema is the Sanskrit word for love, but it is hard to imagine how a coming Sai Avatar can surpass the present Sai in Prema.

The four-floor museum is a stately building in Oriental temple style. It is situated on the top of a hill and commands a lovely view of the serene landscape in the distance framed by a range of hills. Wrought iron entrance gates are guarded by two life-sized elephants in solid black rock, with red cloths painted on their backs. Beautiful white tusks and uplifted trunks greet guests as they enter the grounds.

A museum is usually a rather dull place where one goes to more or less pass the time, so I was greatly surprised to see so much beauty and graciousness within the building. As one enters, one is greeted by the chanting of OM and the lovely perfume of incense. On the ground floor were portrayed the religions of the world and their founders together with their life messages displayed in a fascinating manner. Sophisticated equipment provided music, videos, and films, and everywhere there were flowers to brighten and decorate.

There were many sections with titles written in English and French. One section was about "Creation and the Creator." Another was "The Timeless Teaching about the Self and the Universe." Models in exhibition cases showed scenes from the Mahabharata and the Kurukshetra battle from the Bhagavad Gita. Everything was presented in an exceedingly charming way.

The first floor was devoted to the Sai era. Photos of places and events in his life were shown. In a rotating showcase there were quotations from his teaching such as, "Peace is what everyone seeks, but it can never be secured from the outside world. Peace can only come from the heart of peace within." There was an artistic film with lovely music showing the eternal movements of the sea. Above all, the central message of the Sai Era was underlined — *human unity*.

On the second floor were displayed photos of some of the great European thinkers like Einstein, Schopenhauer, and Max Planck, with quotations from their teachings. It included a large model of the Golden Temple in North India — a marvel of architectural beauty and elegance. The third floor contained an exhibit of musical instruments. You could sit down and pick up earphones to listen to great music from both Eastern and Western masters.

One wonders if there can be any parallel to this grand, colorful, and artistic festive week. A noteworthy feature was the absence of any police force to control the crowd, even with so many high officials present, such as the president of India. Everything was perfectly organized. There was order and the crowds moved in a disciplined manner thanks to the Seva Dals who worked hard for the success of each event. The Supreme Seva Dal was of course the divine himself, giving and giving and serving all of us all the time in the most gracious and loving manner, bearing witness to the fact that without love the world is as barren as the Sahara Desert.

As there are lighthouses constructed in various places in the sea to enable sailors to be aware of rocks and dangers so that they may sail safely, so Sri Sathya Sai Baba is the supreme lighthouse in the sea of worldly existence. He makes us aware of the dangers of indolence, sleep, wandering of mind, attachments to senses. The more easily we follow this light, the safer we are.

A new order of the world is breaking through, however heavy the birth pangs. Hostile forces are still holding on with grim determination. But they can never win the battle. Their end, says Baba, is sure. It is up to us to choose whether we want to belong to the old or follow the new. This is the mission for which Sri Sathya Sai has come—to initiate the new era—which he does with such sublime simplicity and divinity. It is particularly on festival occasions that he comes to be seen by us in all his majesty of heart and soul.

Valedictory Address

The Valedictory address for the Fifth World Conference of the Sri Sathya Sai Seva organizations took place on the day after the 65th birthday celebration, at the Hillview Stadium early in the morning. The air was extraordinarily clear and perfumed, birds were singing, and a sparkling cascade of water fell down over the steep hillside from a reservoir higher up beyond the hill—which is opened up on special occasions. Overlooking all this from the top of the hill was the majestic statue of the victorious Hanuman, the great monkey devotee of Lord Rama, the Avatar.

Throughout the past festival week, heavy thunderstorms had threatened the celebrations, and though one could see the rain all around the horizon pouring down, in the valley the weather had been beautiful and cool. The seven days had passed like a dream.

Now Baba had arrived and was seated in his chair in the center of the stage with special guests on either side. Charm and dignity radiated from his person. A group of college boys, also on the platform, chanted Vedic hymns.

The chairman of the Sathya Sai Organization in the United States said in his speech summing up the conference that as long as we follow Swami's teachings we are happy. We are unhappy if we do not follow them. We should act on these teachings right now, he told us. "Each one of us has a part to play in spreading the dynamic message of Bhagavan

Baba." He added, "There is not a single soul who is going home now unfulfilled."

The central theme of Baba's Valedictory address was love—Prema. Life without love is barren and where there is no love there is no peace, there is no security. He emphasized that it is only through love that you can enjoy and experience Divinity. "If you do not follow this path of love and truth your life will come to ruin. . . . You should not pollute the atmosphere by evil talk and criticism of others," he said.

Baba went on to point out that the three evils of modern society are television, bad literature, and politics. These are the three devils that are destroying the world. Similarly Mother Teresa, in a parallel she drew between Calcutta and New York, once said that poor people in India lack food and shelter but such people can be brought to the godward path very easily, whereas one could not easily treat or help New York people—they have poverty of love and compassion. Their minds are being undermined by television and drugs and their brains are damaged and unreceptive.

Baba explained that Indian culture is extremely special as it embraces all faiths. On the path of love, unity in diversity can be found. When the heart is filled with love, all sins and sorrows are burned away, but dire consequences befall you if you ignore this love. When love goes with you like your own shadow, then God will dwell in you.

To conclude his address, Baba's wonderful deep voice soared high, leading the bhajan Prema Muditha Mana. As my voice joined the million others gathered there singing the bhajan, I felt his message of unity among humankind was translated into a living experience.

The
New Year

The 1991 New Year of the big Indian State Tamil Nadu fell on April 14 and was celebrated by Baba in Kodaikanal. There was a very different scene in 1991 outside Baba's home than in previous years. For the first time since Swami moved into his new house in the mountains in 1985 there were no "reserved" seats nor any litter thrown on the public area outside his residence. Order and cleanliness prevailed everywhere in spite of larger crowds than usual. Devotees were asked to come to Baba's darshans in a disciplined and peaceful way — and so they did, at least within the limits of human nature.

The morning of the Tamil Nadu New Year day began with bhajans in the lovely garden compound, it being big enough to accommodate the many guests who had arrived. Baba's chair was placed in the garden itself, though he was not sitting in it, but standing next to it, keeping time to the music by gentle movements of his hands. The air was cool and clear and felt like a boon after the scorching heat on the plains. The atmosphere was filled with that lovely fragrance which so often announces the divine's presence.

In an opening address to Baba's Tamil Nadu New Year talk, a distinguished member of the Prasanthi Nilayam Trust said, "We are very blessed to live in the lifetime of an avatar who embodies both greatness and goodness. Very often where there is goodness there is no greatness, or where there is greatness there is no goodness. In this avatar we see the rare combination of both qualities." The speaker went on to say, "Today there is total loss of human decency, total loss of respect for elders, of honesty . . . but this avatar has come to avert the catastrophe that is threatening humanity by re-asserting the absolute values. He is ushering in a new age, the Sathya Yuga or the age of Truth. . . . He teaches us every day in a way that even a child can understand. How are we to grasp his divinity, if it were not for his simple yet powerful words which have such a deep impact on us? We can only understand the divine through the cloak of humanity because — as Sri Aurobindo would say — the infinite presence (of the Divine) in its unmitigated splendor would otherwise be too overwhelming for the separate littleness of the limited individual and natural man."

The trust member concluded his talk recalling one of Baba's recent leela's in Prasanthi Nilayam: A mother was sitting in the darshan line with a sick child on her lap. Baba came up to her and asked, "What is the matter with the child?" "Blood cancer," answered the mother with tears in her eyes. Baba then materialized a piece of candy and put it into the mouth of the child. New strength surged through its frail body, it got up and later examinations proved that it had been cured of the dreadful disease. I have myself seen a simi-lar case. It was in Madras. There was a huge crowd. I was sitting next to a poor mother who held a sick child in her arms that was screaming in apparent agony, its face twisted in pain. Swami came out of his house, ignored everybody — even the VIPs sitting next to the place where He eventually was going to be seated — and went straight to the poor mother. Without a word he materialized a piece of candy, and like a mother who gives medicine to her child, with his thumb, he pushed the candy into the mouth of the yelling child. The effect was overwhelming. In an instant, the child's face was lit up in the sweetest and most blissful smile. It sat up on its mother's lap, looking so content and happy, completely relieved from its pain and at peace. The utter simplicity with which Swami brought about this drastic change made a deep impression on me, and I shall never forget it.

Baba's tender heart feels for the poor and their suffering as part of himself; but whether poor or rich he responds immediately to where there is suffering. It is as if he takes the suffering upon himself—you feel completely at peace, like that child. But the relief you feel is often so great that tears come to your eyes out of sheer gratitude.

One time in Kodaikanal, in his absolutely unpretentious way during darshan, he walked up to an American lady sitting in a wheel chair. He asked her to wheel her chair out on the aisle, materialized some vibhuti for her, and told her to put some of it on her tongue and to get up from her wheelchair. She did. With a brisk gait she walked up along the long and narrow aisle, climbed a flight of stairs, and went into the interview room with her husband at her heels. Everybody was clapping her on. A photographer took a photograph of the event. I met her later on in the hotel in Kodaikanal, where we both were staying, and where she freely walked around. I congratulated her on the happy change in her life, and she flashed a sweet, simple smile at me.

To us mortals, Swami's leelas are unfathomable, and they are countless—almost like the stars in the firmament.

There have been several avatars. Not two of them are alike. Each avatar acts according to the need of the time and level of understanding of people when he takes birth. But this Sai avatar has come in what probably is the most corrupt of all times. The corruption is so widespread that it can almost be classified as universal. Matters of the spirit are scoffed at, people are weak in body and mind. *Dharma* (righteousness) is almost nonexistent.

People everywhere are in a sad plight. They feel an inner vacuum that they try to fill with an unbridled pursuit of the urges of the senses. This fails to improve their condition. On the contrary, it drags their minds down into subconscious "mud." The bottom has been reached, but that is often the best place to start to build a new and fresh life.

That summer in Kodaikanal the purpose of Baba's leelas and teachings stood out in all their clarity and luminosity—if there is to be any spiritual upliftment on a universal scale, Baba's leelas are the only way to draw the masses toward a spiritual path. Words about wisdom will no longer do—no one listens. When people, unaware of any higher life and its infinite riches, receive gifts from Swami seemingly taken out of space like rings, vibhuti, or lockets, or when Baba cures cancer simply by saying "cancer is canceled," or brings about thousands upon thousands of cures of incurable diseases which defy medical science, or rescues devotees in danger and disaster—people cannot but feel reverence and devotion for Baba's divine personality. They enter his fold and also a new life by adopting and living the absolute values he teaches. That is the true reason for Baba's leelas and the purpose of his teachings.

But it is also true that thousands of people come to Swami for a cure, but are not cured, for reasons best known to Swami. One may presume that they are insincere or too lazy to affect a change or their lifestyle. The spiritual path is not for lazy people—a cure may even encourage them to be more lazy. There could also be the question of a payment of a karmic debt, in which case "God does not interfere," it has been said.

Sri Aurobindo, himself a great avatar, warns us, "The avatar (Sri Aurobindo) acts according to the need of the leela, not according to a person's idea of what he should or should not do. This is the first principle one must grasp; otherwise one can understand nothing about the manifestation of the Divine."

All Baba's charming leelas prompt us to turn to the spiritual life. When we take one step toward him, he, as he himself says, takes ten steps toward us. This is a fact that has been experienced by innumerable devotees. And the closer we draw to him, the more fully we understand that none but the divine can perform such leelas as he does, nor be so loving as he is. When one first has had a taste of his divinity and its infinite sweetness and blessedness, one has finished with the tastes of the senses, which by comparison seem so vulgar.

An important aspect of Swami's teachings, a point he again and again emphasizes, is to only take pure food. Avoid eating animal food, through which, it has been said by a very wise lady (the Divine Mother of the Sri Aurobindo ashram) one takes in some of the consciousness of the animal one is eating. That type of consumption is not likely to promote spiritual progress.

Swami sows in us the seed of goodness. That is his mission. For we are all devils today, he says. By his loving care and in the light of his divinity those seeds grow up into blossoms and flowers.

It is, however, hard realities that people want in these modern times. They want to be convinced by facts. Baba's leelas are such "hard realities," that help us become aware of his godhood and take us to the path of God.

It is a supreme blessing to be born on Earth when the avatar moves among us, and have the unique opportunity to be guided by him to a true and purposeful life in harmony with the Divine principles—living not outside but inside ourselves. The journey is not too easy, and when there is no guide, then one may become lost on the way. But if we take a guide (Baba) with us, the dangers will be avoided.

Here follows a few quotations from Baba's teachings in Kodaikanal.

"Why have a human life, if you use it only to enjoy the pleasures that animals enjoy? Man has taken human birth to become Divine. Man has to reach the highest plane of consciousness.

"For all things, all people, Truth is the highest authority, the highest ideal. Truth is Brahman. Truth is the Primeval Sound. It is dharma. Truth alone undergoes no change or diminution.

"The heart which has no contentment is like a bamboo basket with holes.

"If you lift the hand to serve, to help, to console, to encourage another human you are lifting it to God, because God is in every person. Be of service to others for that is giving yourself to me. For whatever you give, I will repay you thrice, nay, ten-fold. I will give to those who give of themselves untold joy and bliss, and what is more, lead them by the hand along those petal strewn paths of eternal joy.

"Those who learn the *Sastras* (sacred scriptures of India) and cultivate direct experience can understand Me. Your innate laziness prevents you from the spiritual experience necessary to discover the nature of God. That laziness should go. It is to be driven out.

"The flower of love can blossom in every heart, you need not go in search of the Lord anywhere. There is a small fire emanating from charcoal, which is burning. Charcoal is covered with ash. The ash covers the fire. The Lord resides in your heart, through the power of maya. He is kept out of our vision. If this maya can be removed, then you can get all bliss which ends all sorrows.

"Today what we see in the artistic field is not a desire to do something senseful but anything sensational and sensual, not something noble but anything novel. The literature and cinema of today shows crime and sex, which tingle the nerves and tangle the mind in lust and hatred. What a tragedy.

"Music has been twisted into a stringy mass by the onslaught of the film industry to strangulate the soul's yearnings and stimulate the sensory cravings.

"We cannot always oblige, but we can at least talk obligingly.

"Spiritual knowledge can only be given in silence, like the dew that falls unseen and unheard, yet brings into bloom masses of roses. This has been the gift of India."

This gift of India is today given to us by the Sai Avatar. By a mere silent touch of his hand, he brings into bloom masses of forlorn souls by his sheer love which is deep and vast as the infinite ocean. It is up to us to dive deep into that ocean and collect its precious pearls of *shanti* (peace). After such a dive, one just feels so infinitely grateful that "thou art." It is precisely for that reason that the Sai Avatar has taken birth—that we should come to know our true nature, which is peace born of love and compassion. Peace in us means peace in the world. Do not let us miss the unique chance at this critical hour of human history. We do not know if or when we will get it again.

Epilogue

In a world made mad by wars the stories of Sai are a benediction because they reveal to us something that is eternally fine and good. It is not a display of arrogance and might, of tanks and missiles, but the simple word of a godman to remind us of the greatness that is our true destiny.

If one gives one's mind to Sai and his stories, he is sure to bless you. Reading these stories is in a way keeping his company. The importance of the company of a godman is very great. Sai will be pleased when we attentively read about his leelas and teachings and he will remove our ignorance and poverty of spirit.

One who has his own welfare at heart should apply carefully Sai's message in his own life, then the mind will get rid of its meanness and vain ideas and obtain steadiness. Cast aside sloth and laziness, ward off drowsiness—if we fail to do this, we reduce ourselves to the level of beasts, says the Sai Avatar. Though it looks like he lives in one place, he is present everywhere. This pervasiveness of his is daily experienced by his ashram Prasanthi Nilayam, the Abode of Highest Peace. He is himself, the abode of the Highest Peace, and he transmits the bliss supreme to those who are open to his message of Truth. The whole world is desolate without this Truth.

Glossary

Asuric: hostile

Atma: the Self

Bal Vikas children: children studying Sai Baba's teachings

Bartans: pots and vessels

Bhajans: traditional Indian devotional songs

Bhakti: devotion

Brindavan: the forest of Brinda, near Mathura, where Lord Krishna played as a child

Darsham: the act of grace that allows devotees to see and be in the presence of a Divine personality

Deepavali: the Hindu festival of light

Dharma: right living, right conduct, right action

Divya atma swarupas: embodiments of the divine atma

Ghee: clarified butter

Gopala: another name for Lord Krishna

Govinda: one of the many Indian names for the Divine

Ista: God

Japa: continued repetition of the name of the Lord

Jnana: the embodiment of universal wisdom

Jnani: sage

Kailash: the abode of Lord Shiva

Kuja: an Indian pot

Kurukshetra: the battleground where Arjuna, aided by Krishna, fought the forces of King Dhritarashtra (from the Bhagavad Gita)

Leela: the divine plan or divine sport of the Lord
Lingam: an oval, egg-shape; the symbol of Shiva
Loka is Lokesa: the world is the body of God
Lord Jagannath: Lord of the Universe; another name for
    the Divine
Madhava: divine entity; God
Mahaprasad: sacred food
Mahout: keeper
Manava: human
Mandap: the open area at Whitefield where Baba gives
    darsham
Mandir: temple
Murali: flute
Namaskar: hands raised, palms together on the chest
Namasmarana: constant repetition and reflection on the
    name of the Lord
Padnamaskar: touching the feet of the Divine
Pandal: booth
Pipal tree: the sacred fig tree in India
Prasad: consecrated food, blessed by God
Prasanthi: undisturbed inner peace
Prema: love
Prema Swarupa: embodiment of love
Sadhaka: spiritual aspirant
Sadhana: spiritual practice; spiritual discipline
Sadhu: one who devotes himself or herself to the pursuit of
    truth
Sanathana Dharma: ancient wisdom; the eternal path
Sanathana Sarathi: the ashram magazine
Sankalpa: divine will
Santhi: inner peace
Sanyasi: one who has renounced everything
Sastrasi: sacred scriptures of India
Sathyam: truth
Seva: selfless service
Seva Dal: a volunteer service worker

Shakti: creative power or divine power
Shamiana: patterned canvas
Shanti: peace
Shanti Vedica: the seat of peace
Shivam: auspiciousness
Siddha: one who has attained self-realization
Sishya: aspiring disciple
So'ham Thatwa: I am That; the reality
Sri Venkateswara: another name for Vishnu, the divine
    protector
Sundaram: beauty
Swarupa: nature
Tapa: repetition of the Divine's name
Thali: an auspicious necklace
Vaikunta: heaven
Vairagya: detachment; renunciation
Vedanta: goal of the Vedas; liberation
Veda Purusha: the divine soul
Vibhuti: the sacred ash that Baba produces

Bibliography

Aurobindo, Sri. *Essays on the Gita*. Pondicherry, India: Sri Aurobindo Ashram Trust, 1987. Distributed in the USA by Lotus Light.

_____. *Human Cycle, Ideal of Human Unity, War and Self-Determination*. Pondicherry, India: Sri Aurobindo Ashram Trust, 1985. Distributed in the USA by Lotus Light.

_____. *Letters on Yoga*, 3 volumes. Pondicherry, India: Sri Aurobindo Ashram Trust, 1979. Distributed in the USA by Lotus Light.

_____. *The Life Divine*. Wilmot, WI: Lotus Light Publications, 1990.

_____. *More Lights on Yoga*. Pondicherry, India: Sri Aurobindo Ashram Trust, 1983.

_____. *Savitri: A Legend and a Symbol*. Pondicherry, India: Sri Aurobindo Ashram Trust, 1987. Distributed in the USA by Lotus Light.

_____. *Sri Aurobindo Birth Centenary Library*, 30 volumes. Pondicherry, India: Sri Aurobindo Ashram Trust, 1970–1972. Distributed in the USA by Lotus Light.

_____. *Sri Aurobindo On Himself*. Pondicherry, India: Aurobindo Ashram Trust, 1985. Distributed in the USA by Lotus Light.

Haich, Elisabeth. *Initiation*, translated from German by J. P. Robertson. Redway, CA: Seed Center, 1974.

Kapleau, Philip. *Three Pilars of Zen: Teaching, Practice, Enlightenment*. New York: Doubleday, 1980.

Krystal, Phyllis. *Sai Baba: The Ultimate Experience*. Dorset, UK: Element Books, 1990.

The Mother. *Collected Works of the Mother*, 17 volumes. Pondicherry, India: Sri Aurobindo Ashram Trust, 1979–1991. Distributed in the USA by Lotus Light.

_____. *Prayers and Meditations*. Pondicherry, India: Sri Aurobindo Ashram Trust, 1979. Distributed in the USA by Lotus Light.

Purani, A. B. *Evening Talks with Sri Aurobindo*. Pondicherry, India: Sri Aurobindo Ashram Trust, 1982. Distributed in the USA by Lotus Light.

Yogananda, Paramahansa. *Autobiography of a Yogi*. Los Angeles: Self Realization Fellowship, 1981.

BIRGITTE RODRIGUEZ

The photograph used on the cover of this book shows Sai Baba silhouetted against the sky. He is walking back and forth on the balcony of his Kodaikanal home, His orange robe and black hair contrasting against the sky. He stands and claps His hands in His usual captivating manner, keeping time with the singing and dancing of the Gopis below. As their voices soar upward in a chorus of "Krishna, Krishna, Jai!" He fills them all with his joy and energy.